Marie Webster's
Garden
of
Quilts

WREATH OF ROSES
80 x 94 INCHES. COTTON. MARIE WEBSTER DESIGNED THE WREATH OF ROSES PATTERN IN 1915
AND APPLIQUÉD THIS QUILT IN 1930. THE NAME OF THE QUILTER IS NOT KNOWN.

Collection of Rosalind Webster Perry.

Marie Webster's Garden of Quilts

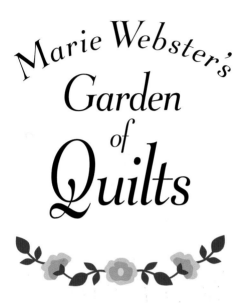

ROSALIND WEBSTER PERRY
AND MARTY FROLLI

with a preface by
CUESTA BENBERRY

PRACTICAL PATCHWORK

Published by
PRACTICAL PATCHWORK
P.O. Box 30065, Santa Barbara, CA 93130
an imprint of Espadaña Press

Library of Congress Control Number: 00-091964

ISBN 0-9620811-8-3

Book designed by The Lily Guild, Santa Barbara, California.
Printed in Canada.

Photo Credits

Bill Boyd: cover, pp. 2, 40, 41, 55, 66, 67
Geoffrey Carr: pp. 88, 89
Wm. B. Dewey: pp. 8, 10, 13, 15
Indianapolis Museum of Art: pp. 60, 65, 102, 103
Scott McClaine: pp. 18, 19, 22 (middle), 23, 24 (middle), 25, 28 (bottom), 54
Myron Miller: pp. 46, 47, 61, 82, 83, 114, 115, 125
Pamela Mougin: pp. 33, 73, 108, 109, 120, 121
Rosalind Perry: p. 27 (middle)
David Roth: back cover (authors)
Tony Valainis: pp. 32, 72
Zehr Photography: pp. 94, 95.

TABLE OF
CONTENTS

This book is dedicated

TO OUR DAUGHTERS

who represent the next generation of quiltmakers

VIRGINIA ELIZABETH PERRY BOBRO

ANGELA MARY PERRY BLADON

MELISSA LYNN FROLLI

MEGHAN ELIZABETH FROLLI

We hope that the love and art of quiltmaking
will continue with them,
their children and
grandchildren.

This is the second book of authentic Marie Webster patterns. The first book, *A Joy Forever,* showcased Marie's early quilts, with 11 of the 12 patterns dating from 1909 to 1917. This sequel, with 14 patterns, encompasses a longer time frame – from her very first appliqué quilt, American Beauty Rose, made about 1908, to her last two designs, Rainbow and Gay Garden, which date from the late 1920s. The variety of designs in this book reveals more clearly her evolution as an artist over the entire span of her career.

Marie sold patterns for her own designs from 1911 to 1942. The patterns in this book are derived from those originals, carefully saved by her daughter-in-law. It has been necessary to remove the seam allowances from Marie's blueprints, and expand the directions from the original one paragraph to include the level of detail expected today.

FOREWORD

Many people have contributed information and illustrations to this project. We are greatly indebted to them all!

First of all, we wish to thank Cuesta Benberry for pioneering the documentation of quilt pattern history and for contributing the preface to this book.

Thanks to Rosalind's mother, Jeanette Scott Thurber, and sister, Katherine Webster Dwight, for generously sharing their memories and their quilts.

To Zetta Hanna, Pat Nicholls (our British consultant), Diane Eardley, and Rosalind's daughters, Virginia Bobro and Angela Bladon,

our appreciation for reading the manuscript and making valuable suggestions.

To our husbands, Mark Frolli and Dick Perry, boundless love and thanks for their encouragement and advice.

For assistance with research and obtaining photos, our thanks go to Debra Ballard; Anita Jones and The Baltimore Museum of Art; Barbara Brackman; Susannah Brown; Nancilu Burdick; Arene W. Burgess; Connie Burke; Hazel Carter; Marguerite Cox; Elsie Dalley; David and Lois Daugherty; Barbara Dirks; Rosamond Eliassen; Jill Sutton Filo; Madonna Fowler; Marilyn Goldman; Joyce Gross; Laurie Hannah, librarian at the Santa Barbara Botanic Garden; Toshiyuki Higuchi, Director of Kokusai Art; Ruby Holt; Virginia McElwain Hueschen; the Indiana Historical Society; the Indianapolis Museum of Art; Jackie Janovsky; Bunnie Jordan and Helen Kelley.

Thanks also to Cheryl Kennedy and the Illinois Quilt Research Project, Land of Lincoln Quilters Association and the Early American Museum (Mahomet, Illinois); Craig Leonard; Barbara Love and the Marion Public Library; Shirley R. McFadden; William F. Munn; Pat L. Nickols; Niloo Paydar, textile curator at the Indianapolis Museum of Art; Dorothy Perry; Jane Przybysz; The Quilters Hall of Fame; Jan Reynolds; Deedee Rietze; Sarah Sebat; Carol Shankel; Nancy Spaulding; Marcy Stanton; Mr. and Mrs. Charles W. Todd, Sr.; Merikay Waldvogel; John Warfel and Jeananne Olsen Wright. And to those we have inadvertently omitted, our apologies and sincere thanks!

The New Patchwork Quilt
By Marie D. Webster

A NEW and artistic note has been achieved in these designs for hand-made quilts of applied patchwork. The aim has been to make them practical as well as beautiful by the use of fast-color linens of good quality in the patterns, and a foundation of equally good white muslin. This "Pink Rose" design with the latticed quilting is charmingly suggestive for a summer cottage bedroom.

THE "Snowflake" quilt design brings to one's imagination the sharp-pointed, glistening snowflakes against a background of blue sky. The quilting in fine stitches simulates the applied pattern, and the border suggests drifts of snow as one sees them after a winter's storm. The quilting in the border is done in curved lines and accentuates this effect of hills and hollows.

IN THIS design the Iris plant has been conventionalized so as to make it consistent with its natural growth—the flowers stretching up in stately array beyond their long-pointed leaves. Here again the quilting pattern follows the flower, and in keeping also with this very striking design is the double striped border in two tones of the violet linen to match the flowers.

THE "Wind-Blown Tulip" design seems to bring a breath of springtime both in form and color. Even the border flowers seem to be waving and nodding their golden heads in the breeze.

NOTE. Transfer patterns cannot be supplied for any of these four quilts, but Mrs. Webster will be glad to answer inquiries regarding them if a stamped, addressed envelope is supplied.

MARIE WEBSTER'S ORIGINAL DESIGNS APPEARED ON THE FIRST COLOR QUILT PAGE IN THE *LADIES' HOME JOURNAL* IN THEIR SPECIAL ISSUE DATED JANUARY 1, 1911. THE QUILTS SHOWN ARE PINK ROSE, SNOWFLAKE, IRIS AND WIND BLOWN TULIP.

Today, Marie D. Webster is recognized as one of the twentieth century's most notable quilt figures. Two of her extraordinary accomplishments were not only personal triumphs, but were also among the primary reasons for Marie Webster's election to The Quilters Hall of Fame. When she wrote the book *Quilts: Their Story and How To Make Them* (1915), based on her research, Webster placed quilts in an historical context, a significant reordering of the manner in which quilts had heretofore been reported.

In previous centuries in America, quilts, largely women's creations, and regardless to how well made or beautiful they were, had not attained the status accorded to valid historical works in the public's view. Webster helped to change that faulty perception when she wrote the first full length quilt history text ever published in America. Her pioneering efforts laid the groundwork on which subsequent quilt history investigations were built.

Perhaps even more influential in the twentieth century were the quilts that resulted from the prodigious quilt designing talents of Marie Webster. She was at the forefront of quilt designers who modernized the American appliqué quilt. Moving away from some popular nineteenth century quilt design concepts such as dense, stylized florals, the vivid red and green palette for botanicals, or heavily embellished silks, satins and velvets, Webster devised distinctly different twentieth century quilts. Her patterns projected an image of simplicity instead of complexity, realism as opposed to stylized or abstracted designs, a clean, airy appearance, and a palette of pastel colors.

Her unmistakable twentieth century quilt designs were immediately appealing to the public, and to other professional quilt designers as well. Numerous professional or commercial sources contemporary to Webster copied her designs outright, or perhaps changed a few lines or so, or gave the design a different title, but with the Webster influence still quite obvious in the finished product. Frequently the copied designs carried no acknowledgment of Webster as the original design source.

PREFACE

Despite embracing such an avant-garde concept as "breaking out of the block" in one of her early quilt patterns, no one could truthfully accuse Marie Webster of being a radical, unconventional quilt designer. She was much too genteel a woman for that. She made all of her innovations and adaptations well within the centuries-old tradition of quiltmaking. Her emphasis on classical beauty and gracefulness is one reason why her quilt designs have captivated quilters for nearly ninety years, and will probably continue to fascinate them for ninety more years. The quilts made from the lovely Marie D. Webster patterns in this book will be cherished now and by succeeding generations. That is a promise.

CUESTA BENBERRY, *Quilt historian and author*

The Baby's Patchwork Quilt

By Marie D. Webster

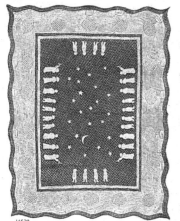

CHILDREN while very young show marked preference for certain toys and little belongings, and could they have pretty quilts for their very own they would surely love them dearly. The quilts shown on this page are practical and sanitary and will give good service, being especially desirable as covers for summer; they also may make more welcome the hour of the Sandman's coming.

The bedtime quilt on the left, with its procession of night-clad children, will be excellent "company" for a tot, to whom a story may be told of the things that sleep near the little trees while the friendly stars keep watch.

The sunbonnet lassies on the right suggest an outing or a call from playmates on the morrow. These lassies may be dressed in bits of the gowns of the little maid, and the quilt thus become a "keepsake quilt."

In quilts of small sizes like these one's inclination is to use dainty materials, such as fine white and colored linen, or possibly fine gingham for the colored parts of the design. The use of gingham for the pattern makes a quilt of lighter weight than when linen is used throughout. And the choice of shades of color sometimes determines the selection. The work consists of applied, not pieced, patterns, and only a thin padding of cotton should be used.

A well-made quilt will last for years and become more attractive as wear softens the colors.

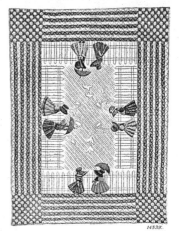

14529
14539

THE wild rose that loves to grow in fragrant, tangled masses by the roadside was made to march in prim rows on the quilt illustrated on the right, to show how pretty it could be on a little bed.

These colorings would be especially attractive in a pink, white and green room, where the bedstead is of white enameled wood or iron. A pillow-slip may be made to match the quilt by applying one of the flowers on each end just above the hem. Finish the edge with crocheted lace or a lace-edged ruffle two inches wide.

IT MUST be "early to bed and early to rise" for the child who would see the sweet morning-glory in all its loveliness, as it must be found before all the dew is gone. Then, too, this delicate flower always curls up and goes to sleep before sunset.

If the pink variety of morning-glory does not harmonize with other decorations in the room the blue varieties of the flower may be used.

If the work is started now, any one of these quilts may easily be finished in time for a Christmas gift to the new baby in the family.

14530

AS GOLDEN butterflies and pansies are so often playmates of little ones in the garden, and beloved by them, they were chosen for the motifs of the pattern on the left. They will carry happy memories of outdoor play to the bedtime hour.

With the quilt on the right teach the little one to tell the petals of the daisy—"loves me, loves me not!"—and many happy moments will be spent in finding out whether the child or his mother loves the more.

In addition to the transfer patterns which may be ordered for these designs I will be glad to answer inquiries about the quilts if a stamped, addressed envelope is inclosed.

TRANSFER patterns— No. 14529, which includes two designs, and No. 14530, which includes three designs—can be supplied, post-free, upon receipt of the price, fifteen cents for each number. Order from your nearest dealer in Ladies' Home Journal patterns; or by mail, giving number of pattern, and inclosing the price to the Pattern Department, The Ladies' Home Journal, Independence Square, Philadelphia, Pennsylvania.

14530

(Page 27)

14530

SIX WEBSTER BABY QUILTS WERE PUBLISHED IN THE *LADIES' HOME JOURNAL*, AUGUST 1912. *TOP:* BEDTIME AND SUNBONNET LASSIES KEEPSAKE QUILT. *CENTER:* WILD ROSE AND MORNING GLORY WREATH. *BOTTOM:* PANSIES & BUTTERFLIES AND DAISY.

Marie Webster loved flowers. When I was a small child and she was over ninety, I used to follow my "Granny" as she strolled through our garden, picking flowers. An avid gardener in her younger days, she filled the yard behind her house in Indiana with daffodils, tulips, lilies and iris. Dogwood and apple trees provided shade.

When she designed her first quilts, Marie naturally turned to her garden for inspiration. She studied the living plants, then gathered blossoms, dried them and traced their shapes, seeking to capture their fragile beauty in fabric.

My grandmother created her quilts for daily use in the home. Lightweight and washable, they lent a fresh and cheerful feeling to the bedroom. But beyond their practical function, they were intended to bring the harmony and beauty of nature into the home. Quilts perfectly expressed her chosen motto, in the words of English poet John Keats, "A thing of beauty is a joy forever."

Marie Webster's work linked the quilting traditions of the 19th century with the new artistic trends of the 20th century. She studied old quilts wherever they were to be found, even hanging out to air on clotheslines in the countryside each spring. She utilized many traditional forms in her quilts, like the central medallion and the four-block set. But her innovative designs were also influenced by the rich artistic currents of the day. The Colonial Revival, Art Nouveau and the Arts and Crafts Movement emerged at the end of the 19th century in reaction to the growing industrialization and depersonalization of society, when machine-made products were rapidly replacing traditional crafts.

The Colonial Revival took shape shortly after the end of the Civil War, and continued to grow in popularity through the 1930s. Many of Marie's quilts evoke an idealized past of the quaint, old-fashioned home and garden, a past brought to life in Alice Morse Earle's books, *Home Life in Colonial Days* (1898) and *Old Time Gardens* (1901).

Exciting Art Nouveau designs, influenced by Japanese art, became popular in America following the Paris Universal Exhibition of 1889. Marie's graceful curving vines and delicately contoured petals reflect Art Nouveau's fascination with organic, sinuous lines.

My Grandmother's Garden of Quilts

ROSALIND WEBSTER PERRY

The Arts and Crafts Movement originated in England in the mid-19th century and began to exert a powerful impact on American taste at the turn of the 20th century. It, too, expressed nostalgia for an earlier time, when individual craftsmen were highly valued for making simple, honest and beautiful objects for everyday use. Marie's quilts, with their sturdy linens and cottons, simple shapes and traditional techniques of hand appliqué and quilting, appealed to those seeking to recapture the virtues of America's pre-industrial past.

MARIE WEBSTER WORKING IN HER GARDEN IN MARION, INDIANA, ABOUT 1915.

By integrating all these new artistic ideas with the time-honored traditions of floral appliqué quilts, Marie brought a fresh new look to the American quilt, inspiring generations of quiltmakers to create their own quilted gardens.

THE FIRST QUILT CELEBRITY

There is a common misconception that the 20th century quilt revival started in the 1920s and that pastel floral appliqué quilts did not become popular until after World War I. In fact, Marie Webster was designing such quilts much earlier. In 1911 and 1912, fourteen of her quilts were published in the leading women's magazine, the *Ladies' Home Journal,* and their patterns were readily available both by mail order and in stores, including the fashionable Marshall Field & Co. of Chicago.

MARIE DAUGHERTY, FIRST PORTRAIT, 1863.

But how did Marie Webster, a woman without a college education or formal art training, born in the mid-19th century, become a famous quilt designer of the 20th century? A traditional stay-at-home wife and mother, she certainly never imagined that she would embark on a career at the age of 50.

Born in 1859, she was the oldest child in a prosperous northern Indiana family whose forebears were early 19th century pioneers. After Marie's marriage in 1884 to businessman George Webster, she resided in Marion, Indiana, raised their son and quietly pursued her interests in reading, history, travel and sewing.

In 1902, after their son left home to attend an eastern college, the couple moved into a newly built Colonial Revival house and Marie turned her attention to its decoration. She searched for a quilt pattern to her liking, but finding none, decided to adapt a traditional Rose of Sharon pattern. Her innovation was to give her version a new, pastel color scheme, in keeping with the natural tones favored by the Arts and Crafts Movement, instead of the bright reds and greens typical of 19th century floral appliqué quilts. Marie probably finished her quilt about 1908. She called it simply Pink Rose, but later renamed it American Beauty Rose.

Encouraged by her family and friends, Marie mailed her new quilt to the *Ladies' Home Journal*, which invited her to submit more designs for their new color features. The first of these quilt pages appeared January 1, 1911, probably the first time that photographs of quilts had ever been published in full color.

Her work proved so popular that her patchwork cushion designs were shown in the August 1911 issue, and 10 more of her quilt designs appeared in the January and August 1912 issues. Eight designs were for full size quilts: Pink Rose, Iris, Snowflake, Wind Blown Tulip, Poppy, Morning Glory, White Dogwood and Sunflower. Six were delightful baby quilts: Pansies and Butterflies, Sunbonnet Lassies, Daisy, Wild Rose, Morning Glory Wreath, and Bedtime.

The New Patchwork Cushions

By Marie D. Webster

A Yellow Rose "Sunshine" Pillow of Linen

A Flower-Basket Quilt Design for a Pillow

The Field Daisy is Pretty on a Green Pillow

The Wild Rose Wreath is a Pleasing Design

A Tulip Design, Formal and Graceful Like the Flower

Sprays of the Iris Flower for Corner Pieces

APPLIQUÉ CUSHION DESIGNS BY MARIE WEBSTER, PUBLISHED IN THE *LADIES' HOME JOURNAL*, AUGUST 1911.

While her first quilt was a variation on a 19th century pattern, her other designs displayed a startling originality. She broke with tradition in her use of color, the naturalism of her flowers and her unique borders. Her most original designs – Poppy, Sunflower, Morning Glory and White Dogwood – have a central focus, rather than an overall repeated block pattern. All of her quilts are noteworthy for their understated elegance, their subtle color schemes and their outstanding workmanship.

Marie Webster became the first quilt celebrity, her name well known to the nearly two million readers of the *Ladies'* *Home Journal*. Soon after her first article appeared in 1911, she began to sell patterns for the quilts. With the help of her son, Lawrence, she developed a unique pattern

MARIE WEBSTER HOLDING BABY LAWRENCE, WITH HER GRANDMOTHER, EMMA BROOKS *(CENTER)*, AND HER MOTHER, MINERVA DAUGHERTY, 1885.

A REVIVAL OF OLD FASHIONED NEEDLE CRAFT

When Mrs. Marie D. Webster contributed patchwork quilt designs with written descriptions to The Ladies' Home Journal *recently she did not anticipate the avalanche of inquiries that would result from it, and the women of the Emily E. Flinn Home have had employment with their needles executing many designs submitted by her to the* Journal. *Mrs. Webster's magazine articles brought inquiries from all over the world, and orders have been sent her from foreign as well as American cities. Her patchwork quilts have created a revival of old fashioned needle craft, and the women of the 'Old Ladies' Home' have profited from it, Mrs. Webster taking orders from inquiries through the mails and bringing the necessary stitching to them. Her patchwork quilts, as published in magazines, have given Mrs. Webster much prestige among those interested in needlecraft. Her quilts have been exhibited in many cities.*

ROLLAND L. WHITSON, *The Centennial History of Grant County, 1914*

packet, containing a blueprint and a tissue paper placement guide, to ensure accuracy in the cutting and placement of the designs. Some of her designs from the *Ladies' Home Journal* were also reprinted by the Home Pattern Company in their 1913 and 1914 catalogs as iron-on transfer patterns or stencils for embroidery.

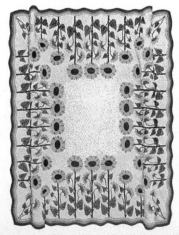

MARIE WEBSTER'S SECOND PAGE OF QUILTS IN THE *LADIES' HOME JOURNAL* APPEARED IN JANUARY 1912, FEATURING POPPY, MORNING GLORY, SUNFLOWER AND WHITE DOGWOOD.

As a rule, Marie did not quilt her own tops, although she may have quilted Pink Rose and the baby quilts herself. Faced with the overwhelming order from the *Ladies' Home Journal* for 13 additional quilts, she turned to the elderly women residing at the local Flinn Home to carry out her quilting designs. However, she loved to plan the quilting. Her favorites were quilted flowers that echoed the appliquéd shapes, with simple diagonals or diamonds filling the background. She sometimes devised novel motifs, like the spider webs on her Sunflower quilt or the picket fence, birds and flowers on her Sunbonnet Lassies baby quilt.

Marie and her quilts traveled widely. A display of her quilts was set up in Chicago's elegant Marshall Field department store to promote the sale of patterns and fabric. According to the *Marion Daily Chronicle* of February 10, 1911, they were given "a prominent position" and were "regarded as the most unique feature of the interesting exhibit which annually attracts many thousands of people to the great store.... Everything halted in the fancy goods department while employees

15

flocked about the striking creations which represent a new development in artistic handiwork."

Marie continued to create inventive new designs. Between 1912 and 1920, she designed and appliquéd Wreath of Roses, Cherokee Rose and Magpie Rose, whose patterns are given in this book, as well as Grapes and Vines, Daffodils and Butterflies, French Baskets, Bunnies, Poinsettia, Clematis in Bloom, and Nasturtium Wreath.

By 1920, she was selling a total of 22 different patterns, with the assistance of her son Lawrence, who drew the blueprints, and her younger sister, Emma Daugherty, who assembled the complicated tissue paper placement guides. Marie worked in a studio on the second floor of her home – a combination office, sewing room and showroom – where she filled orders and showed samples of the patterns and fabrics to customers.

MARIE WEBSTER *(RIGHT)* WITH HER YOUNGER SISTER, EMMA DAUGHERTY, 1934.

A TRUE MASTER

Curiously, it may seem, Marion has become known in more countries, more metropolitan cities, more tiny hamlets, through the art of quilting than through its manufacturers, or any other of its products.

Marion is the home of a world recognized authority on the design, history and making of quilts. Mrs. Marie D. Webster, more locally known as Mrs. George Webster, jr., of South Washington street, and prominent Marion society

woman, has become an outstanding figure in the old art of quilting. Her designs are sought all over the world, and letters come daily from every conceivable person and country, asking advice, designs, instructions, and bits of history....

Day by day letters continue to pour in, indicating that the art of quilting is not a dead or dying one, but that a true master continues to keep it alive for future generations like it has existed since the advent of civilized man.

MARION DAILY CHRONICLE, MAY 28, 1925

Not content with designing and making quilts, Marie's curiosity led her to begin researching and writing about their history as well. After two years of work, her manuscript was accepted by Doubleday, Page & Company. *Quilts: Their Story and How to Make Them* was published in 1915 – the first book entirely devoted to the subject.

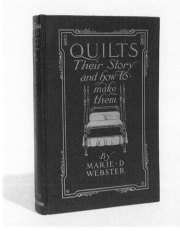

Marie Webster soon gained an international reputation as *the* expert on quilts. Many prominent people corresponded with her and she was invited to lecture at benefits and club meetings. She gave a memorable program, dressed in a flowing green silk gown with an elaborate lace collar. Several friends, also dressed in old-fashioned costumes, would come along to demonstrate quilting techniques, serve tea, and even sing quilting songs!

In 1916, Doubleday reprinted the book and brought out an edition in England. In their 1926 and 1928 editions, four photographs were added to the original 80, including an early illustration of a Hawaiian quilt.

A "DELUX" NUMBERED COPY OF THE FIRST EDITION OF *QUILTS: THEIR STORY AND HOW TO MAKE THEM.*

By 1929, *Quilts: Their Story and How to Make Them* had gone out of print. Marie Webster decided to purchase the printing plates from Doubleday and issue a new printing of 1,000 copies herself. Later, she sold the plates to Tudor Publishing Company of New York, which brought out two more printings in the 1940s.

When I started researching my grandmother's life in 1988, I discovered there was renewed interest in her work. In 1990, adopting the name of my grandmother's quilt kit business, Practical Patchwork, I published a new, expanded edition of *Quilts: Their Story and How to Make Them,* including a biography of the author, extensive notes and additional photographs.

MARIE WEBSTER, ABOUT 1916, IN THE COSTUME SHE WORE FOR HER LECTURES.

From 1911 until 1942, Marie Webster sold unique pattern packets from her home in Marion, Indiana. The distinctive brown envelope was marked with the price, 50 cents, which never increased during those 30 years. Inside the envelope were brief directions, usually illustrated with a photo of the quilt. On the back of the directions were glued several fabric samples, "to show colors used in the original quilt."

In addition, each packet included a blueprint for the appliqué pieces and several full-size tissue paper placement guides, to indicate the correct arrangement of the pieces. These were especially helpful when the flowers were made from several layered petals, as in the Cherokee Rose block shown here.

CHEROKEE ROSE PATTERN TISSUE PAPER GUIDE FOR THE BLOCKS, 8 X 8 INCHES.

MARIE WEBSTER'S PATTERN ENVELOPE.

BLUEPRINT FOR THE CHEROKEE ROSE PATTERN, 5 X 13¼ INCHES, DRAWN BY MARIE WEBSTER'S SON, LAWRENCE.

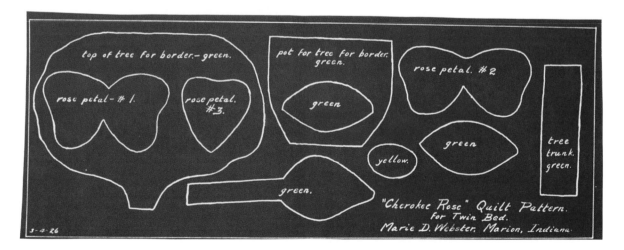

BLUEPRINT FOR THE WIND BLOWN TULIP PATTERN, 8 X 13½ INCHES. MARIE DESIGNED THE PATTERN ABOUT 1910. HER SON, LAWRENCE, PREPARED THIS BLUEPRINT, DATED 9-2-'28.

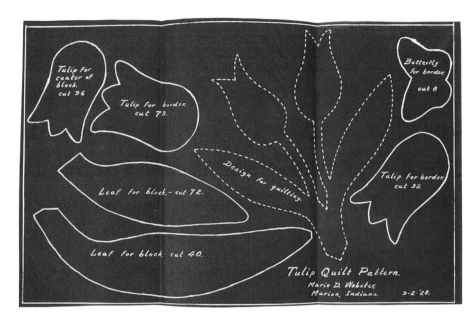

MAGPIE ROSE TISSUE PAPER GUIDE, 11¼ X 22 INCHES, 1916.

GEORGE AND MARIE WEBSTER ARE SHOWN WITH THEIR SON, LAWRENCE, IN THIS PORTRAIT MADE ABOUT 1905.

MAGPIE ROSE PATTERN, FABRIC SWATCHES FROM THE BACK OF THE DIRECTION SHEET, 1916.

Dr. Dunton's Quilt Exhibit

In 1916, Dr. William Rush Dunton, Jr. (1868-1966), a Maryland psychiatrist and pioneer in the development of occupational therapy, invited Marie Webster to lend him some quilts for an exhibit he was planning at the Sheppard and Enoch Pratt Hospital near Baltimore. According to the exhibit labels and photographs in Dr. Dunton's scrapbook (now in The Baltimore Museum of Art), Marie sent six quilts: French Baskets with Daisies, Iris, Wreath of Roses (which Dr. Dunton called "the most beautiful quilt shown"), Bedtime, Sunbonnet Lassies, and Pansies & Butterflies. She also sent a single block from Cherokee Rose, her newest design, and modern Egyptian patchwork panels that were illustrated in her book.

In July 1916, Dr. Dunton purchased Webster quilt patterns to use in his occupational therapy program. A Wind Blown Tulip quilt top, the "first patchwork made by patients" at the hospital, was finished in time to be included in the exhibit in September. Dr. Dunton wrote to Marie: "If you had been on the ward with me this morning and seen the group of ladies who are engaged in making your wind blown tulip I think you will realise that we have already succeeded in arousing some interest. I am very hopeful that the exhibit will arouse still more."

WIND BLOWN TULIP QUILT TOP MADE BY DR. DUNTON'S PATIENTS. *Photos this page courtesy of The Baltimore Museum of Art: Dunton Archives.*

The Revival of Interest in Bed Quilts

To Mrs. Marie D. Webster, of Marion, Indiana, must be given credit for inaugurating the revival of interest in bed quilts and quilting. Her book, Quilts, Their Story and How to Make Them, *was published in 1915, but for several years previously she had published in the* Ladies Home Journal *colored designs for quilts and for quilted pillow tops. The former are reproduced in her book and are chiefly original designs although she has modified some of the older designs making them much more artistic and pleasing....*

WILLIAM AND EDNA DUNTON, "QUILTS AND QUILTING" IN *OCCUPATIONAL THERAPY AND REHABILITATION*, VOL. IX (1931), NO. 3, P. 163.

DR. DUNTON'S QUILT EXHIBIT, SHOWING FOUR QUILTS LOANED BY MARIE WEBSTER. *TOP LEFT,* WREATH OF ROSES; *CENTER,* PANSIES & BUTTERFLIES AND BEDTIME BABY QUILTS; *BOTTOM,* FRENCH BASKETS WITH DAISIES. A PANEL OF EGYPTIAN PATCHWORK FROM HER COLLECTION IS ON THE LEFT.

You are invited to attend an Exhibit of Quilts which will be held at the Sheppard and Enoch Pratt Hospital, Sept. 4 to 9, 1916.

INVITATION TO DR. DUNTON'S QUILT EXHIBIT, PROBABLY PRINTED BY DR. DUNTON'S PATIENTS AS PART OF HIS OCCUPATIONAL THERAPY PROGRAM.

FRENCH BASKETS WITH DAISIES, DESIGNED AND MADE BY MARIE WEBSTER ABOUT 1914, PHOTOGRAPHED BY DR. DUNTON. THE COLORS WERE FRENCH GREY AND WHITE, WITH YELLOW CENTERS FOR THE DAISIES. *Photos this page courtesy of The Baltimore Museum of Art: Dunton Archives.*

ART QUILTS ON DISPLAY
UNIQUE EXHIBITION AT SHEPPARD AND ENOCH PRATT HOSPITAL

An unusual and very interesting exhibition of the quiltmaker's art is being held at the Sheppard and Enoch Pratt Hospital this week. It was arranged by Dr. W. R. Dunton, who has made a study of this sort of handiwork and who has succeeded in gathering some unique specimens for the exhibition.

Some of the quilts are modern, but the majority are antique. Some are of historical importance and others bear the distinction and the marks of having traveled extensively. From Mrs. Marie D. Webster, the designer, of Marion, Ind., Dr. Dunton has secured special types, and with these he intends to instruct the hospital patients in the art of quiltmaking. The work, in fact, has already begun....

BALTIMORE AMERICAN, SEPT. 5, 1916

In the 1920s, Marie Webster continued to design and sell patterns. Two close friends, Evangeline Beshore and Ida Hess, helped her start a new venture, making and selling kits for the Webster designs. Their business, the Practical Patchwork Company, printed a list of "Ready to Make Quilts and Bed Spreads" and later issued a series of more sophisticated 20-page illustrated catalogs. By the mid-1920s, they were selling 17 different quilt and bedspread kits, ranging in price from $5 to $12. In addition to the stamped kits, they also offered basted and finished quilts in the same designs. A basted full-size quilt cost from $27.50 to $37.50, while a fully finished, hand-quilted one cost $65 to $85.

Marie's nine new designs from the 1920s reflect this change in her marketing focus. She started designing specifically for the kit market, by making her patterns easier to appliqué. Six of these designs are included in this book: Cluster of Roses, Dutch Basket, Primrose Wreath, Pink Dogwood in Baskets, Rainbow and Gay Garden. Most of these quilts have scalloped borders and solid color fabrics in shades of yellow, pink, peach, blue and lavender.

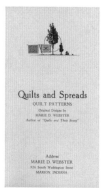

PRACTICAL PATCHWORK CATALOG: COVER AND THE PINK DOGWOOD IN BASKETS PAGE.

The kits were marketed as luxury gift items. In October 1925, *The House Beautiful's* "Window Shopping" column promoted the Webster kits: "These designs are put up in attractive flowered boxes, and would make charming gifts for a bride's shower, as well as wonderful sellers in a gift shop. And, of course, for a woman who likes to do fine sewing no better form could be devised, for, when finished and quilted, one of these spreads is worthy of becoming a valuable and cherished heirloom.... You see they are really works of art. The colors are all fast dyes, and the materials of the very best."

The Practical Patchwork Company sold finished quilts as well as kits, and hired experienced quilters to do this work. The customer who purchased a Webster pattern or kit usually did not do the quilting herself. In fact, the directions actually instruct the quiltmaker to have the top quilted. Customers often asked Marie to recommend a good quilter or to make arrangements for their appliquéd tops to be quilted.

Marie kept the names of quilters from Indiana, Michigan and Kentucky in her address book, listed under the letter "Q." These women typically came from families of modest means, who depended on the extra money earned by quilting.

SARAH HAYS COLE *(LEFT)* AND HER DAUGHTER, DOROTHY COLE SCHLOSSER, OF MARION, INDIANA, PROUDLY DISPLAY THEIR PINK DOGWOOD IN BASKETS QUILT.
Courtesy of Susannah M. Brown.

A MOST PRACTICAL ART

Among the Marion Society women who have discovered that avocations can be made vocations, are the members of the Practical Patchwork company, Mrs. Luther Hess, Mrs. Hiram Beshore and Mrs. George Webster. This company was formed last year and has made such rapid progress that at the present time they are selling their very beautiful and serviceable articles in every part of the United States, through retail stores and private agencies....

Mrs. Hess stated, "Art is best served when charm, beauty and utility are combined by the needle of the housewife in the articles she creates for the comfort and adornment of her home. Patchwork – one of the oldest forms of decoration – can now be so practically applied as to find instant favor with every woman who desires to create beautiful household furnishings of her own without undue effort.

"Not only is it gay and attractive, but patchwork is also a most practical art. Unusual and varied articles suitable for the breakfast nook, the bridge table, and the tea service in the sun-parlor can now be obtained with appropriate decorations formed in this ancient method..."

MARION DAILY CHRONICLE, Nov. 8, 1922

During the Depression, their ability to supplement the family income must have been especially important. They usually charged one cent per yard of quilting thread used. Prices quoted for having a quilt top quilted, including the cost of batting and backing, ranged from $12 to $35, depending on the size of the quilt and the complexity of the quilting designs.

The finest quilters were in great demand. In 1933, Marie replied to a customer's inquiry, "At present my good quilters are busy, with orders ahead, so it will be impossible to do your quilts before the holidays...." She suggested that the customer contact Anne Orr of Tennessee, who also ran a successful kit and pattern business. By 1940, it was becoming so difficult to find good quilters that Marie referred a potential customer to quilt shop owner Mary McElwain, saying, "The quilter here has just moved out of the state and I have found no one as yet to do quilting... I shall be pleased to advise you if I learn of a good quilter here."

ONE BLOCK FROM A PRACTICAL PATCHWORK KIT FOR PINK DOGWOOD IN BASKETS, 14 x 25 INCHES. THE REVERSE SHOWS THE LINES STAMPED ON THE FABRIC TO AID IN THE PLACEMENT OF THE APPLIQUÉ.
Courtesy of The Quilters Hall of Fame.

Marie Webster and her friends packaged their kits in beautiful boxes printed with flowers, spider webs and butterflies. Included in the box was all the fabric needed for the blocks and borders, marked with dotted lines to show where the design was to be appliquéd. The petals, leaves and other pieces were marked on various solid color fabrics, ready to cut out, baste and appliqué in place. The popular "Genuine Peter Pan Guaranteed Fast Color Wash Fabrics" were preferred.

The boxed kit illustrated on page 25 is for French Baskets with Roses, designed about 1914. However, the kit dates from the 1920s or 30s. Included in the kit were samples intended to demonstrate the techniques required to complete the quilt. One of

the white baskets was slit along a marked line, then the edges turned under and basted, to demonstrate the technique of reverse appliqué. Rose petal shapes were pinned onto one of the blue blocks, to show the correct layering of the petals and flower center. Pieces of blue and white fabric were marked with lines for cutting the bias strips, and short sections were cut, folded and basted, to show how it should be done.

This kit was part of the inventory of Louis Levy's furniture store in Ligonier, Indiana. Lou's wife, Ruth, ran a gift shop in one section of the store, selling quilt kits as well as baby clothes and embroidery supplies. Ruth and her mother, Mahalia Yoder Todd (1868-1938), made several quilts from Webster patterns and kits.

FRENCH BASKETS WITH ROSES, DETAIL. THE NAME OF THE QUILTMAKER IS NOT KNOWN.
Collection of Rosalind W. Perry.

RUTH TODD LEVY (1893-1989).
Courtesy of Ruth Todd Levy's nephew, Charles W. Todd, Sr.

LOU LEVY'S STORE IN LIGONIER, INDIANA, WHERE HIS WIFE RUTH SOLD WEBSTER PATTERNS AND KITS.
Courtesy of Charles W. Todd, Sr.

PRACTICAL PATCHWORK GIFT BOX
FOR A FRENCH BASKETS KIT,
CONTAINING PRE-MARKED FABRIC.
THIS KIT WAS IN THE INVENTORY
OF RUTH LEVY'S GIFT SHOP IN
LIGONIER, INDIANA.
Collection of Dorothy Perry.

MAGPIE ROSE
72 X 81 INCHES.
DESIGNED BY MARIE
WEBSTER AND MADE BY
RUTH LEVY IN LIGONIER,
INDIANA, ABOUT 1930.
RUTH'S MOTHER,
MAHALIA YODER TODD,
MAY HAVE QUILTED IT.
Collection of Dorothy Perry.

MARY MCELWAIN'S QUILT SHOP IN WALWORTH, WISCONSIN. SIX MARIE WEBSTER DESIGNS APPEAR IN THIS VIEW. *LEFT TO RIGHT:* RAINBOW PILLOW (ON SHELF); SNOWFLAKE (FOLDED ON TABLE); BUNNIES (BETWEEN OVERALL BOYS AND SUNBONNET SUE); DUTCH BASKET (DRAPED OVER A FRAME); PRIMROSE WREATH (ABOVE DUTCH BASKET) AND DAISY (FAR RIGHT, BEHIND THE BASKET QUILT). THIS PHOTO APPEARED IN MARY MCELWAIN'S CATALOG OF QUILT PATTERNS, *ROMANCE OF THE VILLAGE QUILTS*, IN 1936. *Courtesy of Mary McElwain's granddaughter, Virginia McElwain Hueschen.*

SOMETHING TO CHERISH ALWAYS

Patchwork – one of the oldest forms of decoration – combines charm, beauty and utility in the Quilts and Spreads which we offer to those interested in fine needlework. Aside from the sentiment attached to heirlooms, which make all Quilts desirable, there must be real value, which in a Quilt is achieved by workmanship, quality of material and harmonious color.

When you have made a Quilt or Spread designed by Marie D. Webster, who is recognized throughout the entire country as a quilt authority, you will have something to cherish always.

MARY A. MCELWAIN, *ROMANCE OF THE VILLAGE QUILTS*, 1936

When Marie reached the age of 70, she began to cut back on her quilting activities, in part because of her husband George's poor health. She no longer created new designs, but continued to fill orders for her patterns.

After the Webster family moved to New Jersey in 1942, her friends, Evangeline Beshore, Ida (Hess) Lillard and Gloria Eward, kept the kit business going for another few years. The last known reference to the Practical Patchwork Company is in a letter Marie wrote in 1946 to famous quiltmaker Bertha Stenge: "When I moved here four years ago I left my quilt interests in Marion with the Practical Patchwork Company.... They use my designs for stamping quilts and can arrange for quilting."

Sharing a home with her son's family in New Jersey, she lived quietly in retirement until her death in 1956 – her achievements all but forgotten. But with the growing revival of interest in quilts in the 1970s and 80s, her work gained a new audience and a new appreciation.

In 1991, the first retrospective of her quilts was organized by the Indianapolis Museum of Art. This exhibit then traveled from coast to coast, visiting the American Museum of Quilts and Textiles in California (1992), The Great American Quilt Festival of the Museum of American Folk Art in New York City (1993), and the Spencer Museum of Art in Lawrence, Kansas (1994). In 1998, the Webster quilts crossed the Pacific for a tour of four Japanese cities, where they were viewed by 64,000 enthusiastic quilt lovers. The exhibit, titled "American Applique Quilt," was sponsored by Kokusai Art and included quilts by Rose Kretsinger and other contemporaries of Marie Webster.

The year 1991 also marked the date of Marie Webster's induction into The Quilters Hall of Fame, which later acquired the home where the Websters lived from 1902 to 1942. In 1993, Marie Webster House was declared a National Historic Landmark and a Landmark Site of Women's History, the first official recognition of a quiltmaker as a significant figure in American cultural history. Complete renovation of the home is underway to prepare for its rebirth as the museum of The Quilters Hall of Fame.

POSTER FOR THE EXHIBIT OF WEBSTER QUILTS AT THE HANKYU MUSEUM IN KOBE, JAPAN, 1998.
Courtesy of Kobe Hankyu Museum.

There is no doubt that Marie Webster played a major role in setting the course of American quilt design in the early 20th century. Countless patterns that appeared between 1911 and 1950 were inspired by her ideas. A central focus, naturally contoured flowers, plain solid pastels on a light background and scalloped borders – all were made popular by her designs.

And now, we invite you to select your favorite Marie Webster pattern and join the world-wide community of quiltmakers who have enjoyed making and displaying these lovely designs for nearly a century!

The Quilters Hall of Fame was founded in 1979 to pay tribute to individuals who have made outstanding contributions to the world of quilting. The home of Marie Webster, who was inducted in 1991, has been chosen for the headquarters and museum of The Quilters Hall of Fame. This handsome, century-old residence was designated a National Historic Landmark in 1993.

Quilt lovers from across the country have contributed to this project honoring our quilting heritage. For more information about The Quilters Hall of Fame and Marie Webster House, please write to P.O. Box 681, Marion, IN 46952.

MARIE WEBSTER HOUSE, 926 SOUTH WASHINGTON STREET, MARION, INDIANA, WHERE THE FAMILY LIVED FROM 1902 TO 1942. *ABOVE*, AS IT APPEARED ABOUT 1905; *BELOW*, IN 1996 WHILE EXTENSIVE RENOVATION WAS IN PROGRESS FOR THE QUILTERS HALL OF FAME.

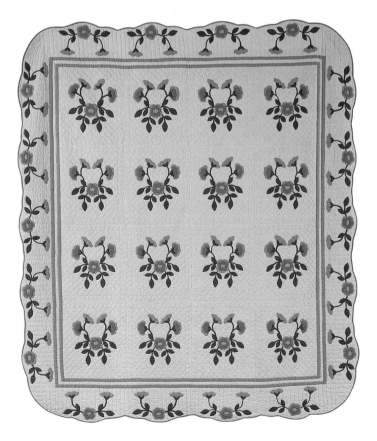

WAYSIDE ROSES, 80 X 98 INCHES. MADE IN 1998-99 BY 67 MEMBERS OF THE BALTIMORE APPLIQUÉ SOCIETY AND DONATED TO THE QUILTERS HALL OF FAME. JACKIE JANOVSKY DRAFTED THE PATTERN, USING MARIE WEBSTER'S ORIGINAL PATTERN. IT WAS HAND QUILTED BY BELLWEATHER QUILTS.
Courtesy of The Quilters Hall of Fame.

The
Patterns

BASIC INFORMATION

❧ FABRIC

• All of the patterns in this book use only solid color fabrics, except Magpie Rose and Cherokee Rose. When choosing light colored solids, avoid thin cottons which will allow the seam allowances to shadow through.

• Yardage calculations are based on 45″ wide fabric. Check the width of all fabrics before purchasing. Recalculate yardage if width is less than 45″.

❧ CUTTING

• Yardage given allows for cutting all borders along the lengthwise grain of the fabric. In some instances, you may save fabric by cutting borders on the cross-grain, but if you do this then you must recalculate the yardage.

• When both borders and appliqué pieces are to be cut from the same piece of fabric, first cut the borders along the lengthwise grain and then cut the appliqué pieces from the remaining fabric.

• Exact measurements have been given for background squares, rectangles and borders. However, since appliqué often shrinks and distorts the shape of the background, it is suggested that you cut all background pieces slightly larger than needed. Complete appliqué, then cut background to exact size.

• When cutting appliqué pieces, always add a turn-under allowance. We have allowed enough yardage for a ¼″ turn-under allowance. When appliquéing small pieces, you may prefer a narrower turn-under allowance.

• The binding on Marie Webster's quilts is a very narrow single fold bias, with a finished width of either ¼″ or ⅜″. We have calculated yardage based on the binding width listed for each quilt. Today's quilters often use double fold, ½″ wide finished binding to strengthen the outside edges. If you choose to make a wider binding, remember to recalculate the yardage.

❧ APPLIQUÉ

• Marie Webster used hand appliqué with a very narrow turn-under allowance. First she prepared the pieces by basting the turn-under allowances. Then she basted the pieces to the background. The appliqué was done in very fine hemstitch.

• Some appliqué pieces in Dutch Basket, Cluster of Roses and Magpie Rose require reverse appliqué, where a portion of an upper layer of fabric is cut away and turned under to expose a lower layer of fabric. This technique adds an interesting effect to the roses in these three quilts and to the baskets in Dutch Basket. Consult the assembly instructions for detailed information.

Diagonals   *Double diagonals*

30

• Today, many different methods of appliqué are used, such as needle-turn appliqué and freezer paper appliqué. Consult the Suggested Reading list for books which describe a variety of techniques.

• When appliquéing the quilt blocks, you may find it helpful to hand crease each background piece across the center – horizontally, vertically and diagonally. Lightly mark the design on the background for positioning.

• Some quilts include stems made of bias strips. Depending on the finished width desired, cut the bias either ⅝″ or ¾″ wide, then fold in thirds and baste. Pin or baste stems in place, easing the bias around curves. Appliqué along both sides, tucking the ends under leaves and flowers wherever possible.

• Marie's appliqué pieces often include difficult points and sharp angles – a challenge for any quilter! You may need to practice before tackling some of these patterns. For best results, as Marie once said, your stitches should be "so tiny that a magnifying glass would be required to discover them!"

 ## ASSEMBLY

• Use a ¼″ seam allowance when assembling the quilt top.

• When blocks are set straight, as in Wind Blown Tulip and Wreath of Roses, sew rows of blocks together and then sew the rows together to complete the quilt top.

• When blocks are set on point, as in Cherokee Rose, sew the diagonal rows together and then sew the rows together.

BATTING

• Marie Webster always used a very thin cotton batting, for a lightweight and elegant quilt. Today, you can achieve the same effect by choosing either 100% cotton, cotton/polyester or light polyester batting.

QUILTING

• The quilting on these quilts is both extensive and beautiful. In most cases, Marie hired other women to do the quilting to her specifications. She often used variations of her appliqué designs for quilting templates, as in Wind Blown Tulip and Morning Glory.

• Close quilting was necessary to secure the cotton batting, with quilting lines sometimes only ¼″ or even ⅛″ apart. Simple background designs were preferred, like those shown here.

Diamonds

Hanging diamonds

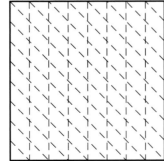

AMERICAN BEAUTY ROSE. 86 x 87 INCHES. COTTON AND LINEN. DESIGNED AND MADE BY MARIE WEBSTER, ABOUT 1908.
THIS IS MARIE WEBSTER'S FIRST APPLIQUÉ QUILT, ORIGINALLY CALLED PINK ROSE.

Indianapolis Museum of Art from the Collection of Marie Daugherty Webster,

Gift of the Shelburne Museum, Shelburne, Vermont.

This is the quilt that started Marie Webster's rise to fame! We do not know exactly when she began to design and make it , but about 1908, she mailed the finished quilt to the offices of the *Ladies' Home Journal* in Philadelphia. When the magazine editor, Edward Bok, decided to publish it, he invited Marie to design more quilts – enough to fill a whole page with new quilt designs, in stunning full color. Her Rose quilt, together with Iris, Wind Blown Tulip and Snowflake, were featured in the magazine's special New Year's number of January 1, 1911 (1/1/11).

A beautiful example of the Colonial Revival style, Marie's quilt reinvents a 19th century Rose of Sharon design in a new 20th century pastel color scheme. It contains many features which would become immensely popular in the 1920s and 1930s – a symmetrical, balanced, and integrated design, and a subtly shaded palette of solid color fabrics.

Although this is Marie's most traditional design, it incorporates some innovations. Instead

AMERICAN BEAUTY ROSE

of one block repeated 16 times, there are 3 variations depending on the block's position, labeled Block a, Block b and Block c.

In Block a, the rose is surrounded by 4 trellis pieces. This block is repeated 4 times in the center of the quilt. There are 8 Block b, 2 on each side. In each Block b, there are 3 trellis pieces and a single bud, placed on the side of the block nearest the border. The third variant, Block c, containing 2 trellis pieces and 2 buds, is placed in the 4 corners. The trellis serves to weave the individual flower blocks into a unified design.

When Marie Webster first offered the pattern for sale, she called it simply Rose Quilt or Pink Rose. In the 1920s, she renamed it American Beauty Rose for a popular French hybrid rose. This rose variety was originally named Mme Ferdinand Jamin, but in 1885, its name was changed to American Beauty Rose, to appeal to the American market.

This variety proved difficult to grow in home gardens, but became successful commercially because of its large deep rich pink blossoms, its beautiful fragrance and stiff, straight stems.

"A new and artistic note has been achieved in these designs for hand-made quilts of applied patchwork. The aim has been to make them practical as well as beautiful by the use of fast-color linens of good quality.... This 'Pink Rose' design with the latticed quilting is charmingly suggestive for a summer cottage bedroom."

LADIES' HOME JOURNAL, JANUARY 1, 1911

AMERICAN BEAUTY ROSE *pattern*

FINISHED SIZES

Quilt: 89″ x 89″

Blocks: 16½″ x 16½″

Borders: 11½″ wide

Binding: ¼″ wide

YARDAGE

10 yards white for background and borders

1½ yards light pink for roses and swags

2 yards medium pink for roses, buds and swags

1¼ yards dark pink for roses and buds

1 yard light green for trellis

2¼ yards dark green for leaves, calyxes and swags

9 yards for backing

¾ yard dark green for binding

White
Cut 10 yards into 2 pieces:
    4 yards and 6 yards.
From 4 yards,
    cut 16 squares 17″ x 17″.
From 6 yards,
    cut 4 borders 12″ x 89½″.

Light Pink
16 A rose petals
16 O swags

Medium Pink
16 B rose petals
16 D rose centers
16 F small buds
16 G split buds
16 N swags

Dark Pink
16 C rose petals
16 E large buds
8 F small buds

Light Green
48 T trellises

Dark Green
4 H large calyxes
4 H large calyxes reversed
16 J small calyxes
64 K leaf/stems
128 L1 large leaves
128 L2 small leaves
16 M leaves
16 P swags

Backing
Cut 9 yards into three 3-yard lengths.
Seam lengthwise.

Binding
Cut bias strips 1¼″ wide for ¼″
finished single fold binding.

1. Referring to the Block Diagrams, make 4 Block a, 8 Block b and 4 Block c. Referring to the Placement Diagram, complete appliqué on the blocks. Appliqué T trellises first, aligning center of trellis with center of block edge. Next appliqué the F buds, J calyxes, K leaf/stems, L1 large leaves and L2 small leaves. Last, appliqué a rose unit (A, B, C rose petals and D rose center) in the center of each block. To reduce bulk, you may wish to trim the extra fabric under each rose petal as you complete the appliqué.

2. Referring to the Placement Diagram, complete appliqué on 4 borders. Appliqué N, O, and P swags first. There is no need to turn under the long curved edges of swags O and P, as they will be positioned under the adjacent swag. Appliqué a border bud unit (1 E bud, 1 G split bud and 1M leaf) where the swag units meet. Corner bud units will be appliquéd over the mitered seam, after quilt top has been assembled.

3. Referring to the full quilt diagram, assemble 16 blocks. Note placement of blocks to achieve a uniform trellis pattern. Add borders, aligning the border bud units with the block seams. Miter border corner seams. Appliqué corner bud units (1 E bud, 1 G split bud, 1 M leaf, 2 F buds, 1 H calyx and 1 H calyx reversed) over the mitered seams.

4. Layer quilt top, batting and backing, then baste.

5. Quilt around outside of all appliquéd pieces. Quilt background with small diamonds.

6. Bind quilt with dark green.

Block a

Block b

Block c

Placement Diagram

A

B

C

D

Trellis
T

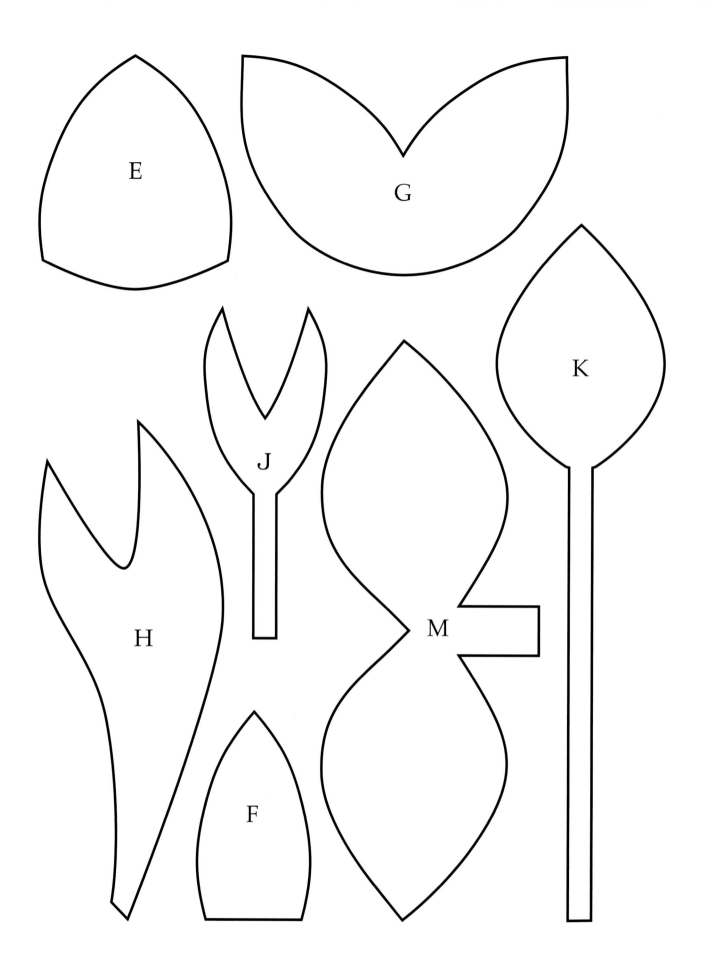

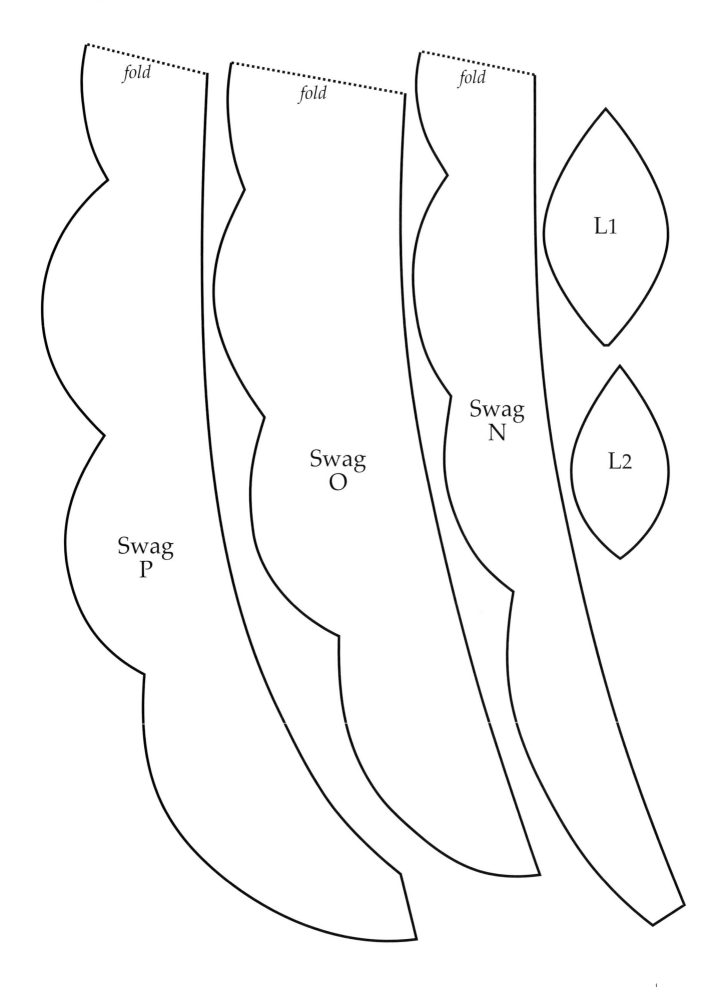

fold

fold

fold

Swag
P

Swag
O

Swag
N

L1

L2

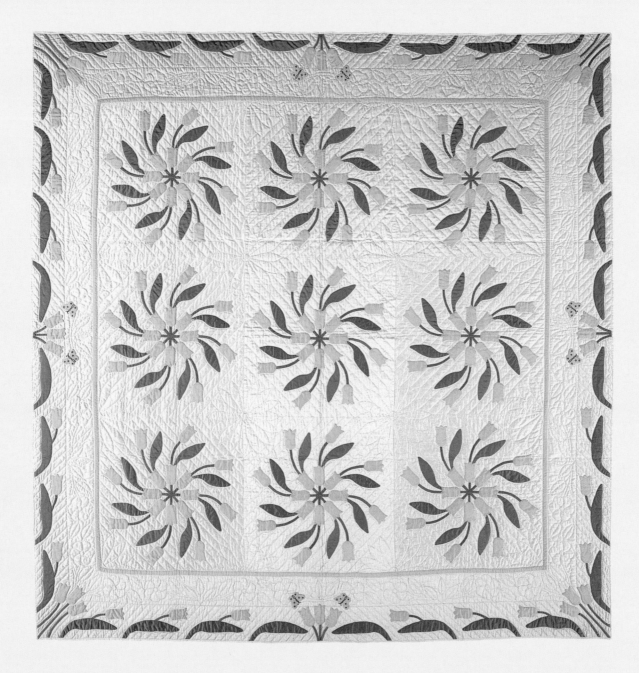

WIND BLOWN TULIP. 80 x 80 INCHES. COTTON. THIS QUILT WAS MADE FROM MARIE WEBSTER'S PATTERN BY AN UNKNOWN QUILTMAKER. IT IS FAITHFUL TO THE ORIGINAL PATTERN, RATHER THAN THE LATER MOUNTAIN MIST VERSION, FOR IT INCLUDES THE BUTTERFLIES AND THE TRIPLE TULIP CLUSTERS OF MARIE'S DESIGN. THE FABRIC IS A LOVELY SOFT SATEEN. THE QUILTING AND BINDING MAY HAVE BEEN ADDED LATER.

Collection of Rosalind Webster Perry.

Wind Blown Tulip has been a favorite of quiltmakers since it first appeared in the *Ladies' Home Journal* in January 1911. While Marie's pattern was inspired by a traditional Pennsylvania Dutch folk art design of swirling tulips, the graceful border of "fallen tulips" is entirely her own invention.

The Stearns & Foster Company popularized a variation of the Webster pattern. "The Wind-blown Tulip" (design J) was among the first patterns pictured on their Mountain Mist batting wrapper in 1929, and has continued to appear on their pattern list down to the present day. Stearns & Foster also adapted Webster designs for their Sunflower, Dogwood and Dancing Daffodil patterns, without acknowledging Marie Webster as their source.

Stearns & Foster introduced several

WIND BLOWN TULIP

minor changes in the Wind Blown Tulip design, which distinguish quilts made from the Mountain Mist pattern from quilts made from the earlier Webster pattern. The Stearns & Foster pattern omitted the butterflies and substituted a single tulip for the clusters of three flowers in the border. In addition, they changed the colors, added three blocks to make it a twelve-block quilt, and reversed the border flowers so they bend toward the corners instead of toward the center of each side. It is this variation that is usually seen, since the Mountain Mist patterns were more widely distributed than the Webster patterns.

We are proud to present the authentic Marie Webster pattern, which has not been available since she stopped selling patterns in 1942. We hope you enjoy making your very own Wind Blown Tulip!

> *" The 'Wind Blown Tulip' design seems to bring a breath of springtime both in form and colour. Even the border flowers seem to be waving and nodding their golden heads in the breeze."*
>
> LADIES' HOME JOURNAL, JANUARY 1, 1911

WIND BLOWN TULIP *pattern*

FINISHED SIZES

Quilt: 87½″ x 87½″

Blocks: 22″ x 22″

Borders:

  1¼″ wide light yellow or pink

  1¼″ wide white

  1¼″ wide dark yellow or pink

  7″ wide white

Binding: ¼″ wide

YARDAGE

9 yards white for background and borders

2 yards light yellow or pink for tulips and
    narrow border

2¼ yards dark yellow or pink for tulips and
    narrow border

3 yards green for leaves and stems

9 yards for backing

¾ yard green for binding

White

Cut 9 yards into 2 pieces:
>   6 yards and 3 yards.

From 6 yards,
>   cut 9 squares 22½" x 22½".

From 3 yards, cut:
>   4 narrow borders 1¼" x 71½"
>   4 outer borders 7½" x 88"

Light yellow or pink

4 narrow borders 1¾" x 69"
24 A tulips for borders
72 B tulips for blocks
8 D butterflies for borders

Dark yellow or pink

4 narrow borders 1¾" x 74"
72 A tulips for blocks
32 C tulips for borders

Green

Cut 3 yards into 2 pieces:
>   2 yards and 1 yard.

From 2 yards cut:
>   72 L1 leaves for blocks
>   40 L2 leaves for borders

From 1 yard, cut ¾" wide
>   bias strips for stems.

Backing

Cut 9 yards into
three 3-yard pieces.
Seam lengthwise.

Binding

Cut bias strips 1¼" wide
for ¼" finished single
fold binding.

1. Referring to the Placement Diagram, complete appliqué on 9 blocks. Appliqué bias stems first. Arrange 4 stems so that they cross in the center of each block. Next appliqué 8 L1 leaves, 8 dark A tulips and 8 light B tulips.

2. Complete appliqué on borders, referring to the Placement Diagram. Appliqué bias stems first. Next appliqué L2 leaves, dark C tulips, light A tulips and D butterflies. Complete appliqué at border corners after sewing borders to quilt top.

3. Stitch together the 9 appliquéd blocks as shown. Sew light narrow borders, white narrow borders and dark narrow borders together lengthwise. Stitch narrow borders to block unit, mitering the corner seams. Add appliquéd outer border, mitering the corner seams. Complete appliqué at corners.

4. Layer quilt top, batting and backing, then baste.

5. Quilt around outside of all appliquéd pieces. Place the quilting design in the corners of each block. Quilt remaining areas as desired.

6. Bind quilt with green.

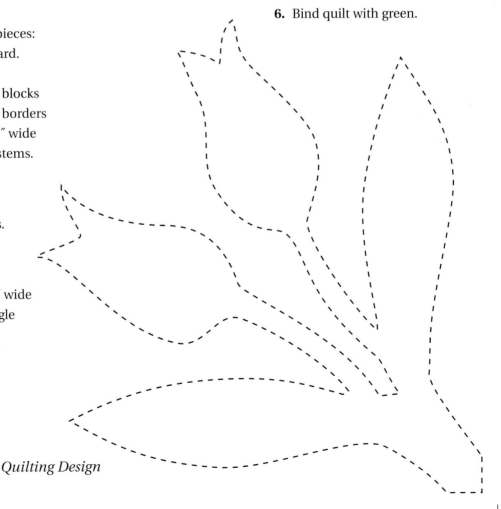

Quilting Design

Placement Diagram

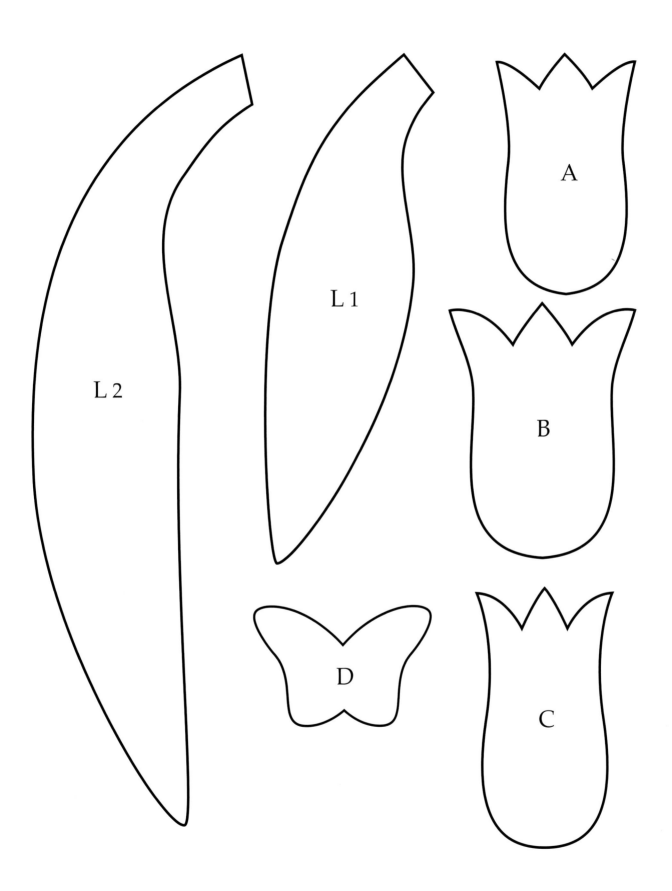

MORNING GLORY. 84 x 84 INCHES. COTTON AND LINEN. MARIE WEBSTER DESIGNED AND APPLIQUÉD
THIS BEAUTIFUL QUILT FOR THE *LADIES' HOME JOURNAL* FEATURE OF JANUARY 1912. IT WAS PROBABLY
QUILTED BY RESIDENTS OF THE EMILY FLINN MEMORIAL HOME IN MARION, INDIANA.

Collection of Katherine Webster Dwight.

This lovely quilt evokes the old-fashioned or "colonial" flower garden, as it was idealized at the beginning of the 20th century. Marie's pattern brochure emphasized the "dainty flowers arranged with leaves and buds in graceful trailing vines," the perfect blossoms to frame the doorway of a quaint country cottage.

This is one of Marie Webster's earliest quilts. She made it about 1910 for the *Ladies' Home Journal*, where it was published in their January 1912 issue, together with three of her most innovative designs: Poppy, White Dogwood and Sunflower. As in many of her early quilts, she chose soft pastel linen fabrics for the appliqué – three shades of blue for the flowers and buds, with just one shade of green for all the leaves and gently curving vines.

The design is both intriguing and ingenious. Although Marie has created the effect of a whole cloth quilt, the design actually consists of 25 blocks, forming two concentric wreaths within an appliquéd border. There are three different block arrangements, labeled Block a, Block b and Block c. Eight of each will be needed to make the complete design, plus one plain block for the center, to be quilted with a morning glory motif.

The appliquéd border features sprays of morning glories, which echo the flowing lines of the central wreaths. The entire quilt is simply framed by a pieced border of blue and white one-inch squares, within a narrow outer blue border.

The center block is quilted with a wreath of morning glories. The rest of the quilting is simple and geometrical, but intense. Quarter-inch diamonds form the overall background design, with diagonal lines at ⅝ inch intervals in the border area.

MORNING GLORY

> "*Morning Glories, in one of their many beautiful and delicate varieties, were chosen for this quilt, and while the design is conventional to a certain extent, it holds much of the natural grace of the growing vine.*"
>
> LADIES' HOME JOURNAL, JANUARY 1912

MORNING GLORY *pattern*

FINISHED SIZES

Quilt: 86″ x 86″

Blocks: 14″ x 14″

White border: 6″ wide

Pieced border: 1″ wide

Outer blue border: 1″ wide

Binding: ¼″ wide

YARDAGE

8½ yards white for blocks and borders

2½ yards light blue for flowers, buds and borders

¾ yard medium blue for flowers and buds

¾ yard dark blue for flowers and buds

3½ yards green for leaves, calyxes, stems and vines

9 yards for backing

¾ yard medium blue for binding

White

Cut 8½ yards into 2 pieces:

    2½ yards and 6 yards

From 2½ yards cut:

    2 borders 6½″ x 70½″

    2 borders 6½″ x 82½″

    4 strips 1½″ wide x 2½ yards,

        for pieced borders

From 6 yards, cut 25 squares

    14½″ x 14½″.

Light blue

2 borders 1½″ x 84½″

2 borders 1½″ x 86½″

4 strips 1½″ wide x 2½ yards,

    for pieced borders.

24 A flowers

40 B flowers

48 D buds

Medium blue

16 A flowers, 8 C flowers, 48 D buds

Dark blue

8 A flowers, 12 B flowers,

8 E flower bases, 72 D buds

Green

Cut 3½ yards into 2 pieces:

    2¼ yards and 1¼ yards

From 2¼ yards cut:

    32 G leaves, 100 H leaves,

    276 F calyxes (on bias)

For added interest, you may cut half of the leaves reversed.

From 1¼ yards, cut ¾″ wide bias strips for vines and stems.

Backing

Cut 9 yards into three 3-yard pieces. Seam lengthwise.

Binding

Cut bias strips 1¼″ wide for ¼″ finished single fold binding.

1. There are 25 blocks: 24 appliquéd and one plain block in the center. Referring to the Placement Diagrams, prepare Blocks a, b and c for appliqué. For vines and stems, fold ¾″ wide bias into thirds lengthwise. Use small section of the bias strips for the stems. Vines, stems and calyxes can be arched into pleasing curves, because the pieces have been cut on the bias.

For the continuous vines, carefully mark their placement on each block. Referring to the Placement Diagrams, note that the vines meet at the sides of the blocks, at a point 6½″ from the inner edge of the finished 14″ block. Vines are appliquéd onto individual blocks. The ends of the vines on adjoining blocks are caught in the common seam.

First appliqué the flowers, buds and stems. Next appliqué calyxes and leaves. Note that the flowers and buds are covered by the F calyxes. The leaves cover the stems. Last, appliqué the vine.

2. Referring to the Border and Border Corner Placement Diagrams, complete appliqué on borders. At the border corners, finish the appliqué of the vine and flower clusters after the borders have been sewn to the blocks.

3. Referring to the Block Assembly Diagram, sew together the 24 appliquéd blocks and one plain center block. Add appliquéd borders. Complete appliqué at the border corners.

4. Referring to the Pieced Border Diagram, sew together 4 white and 4 light blue strips, along the long sides, alternating the white and light blue strips. Cut across the sewn unit every 1½″. Sew units together to make 2 pieced borders, 1½″ x 82½″ and 2 pieced borders 1½″ x 84½″. Add pieced borders to quilt top.

5. Add light blue outer borders.

6. Layer quilt top, batting and backing, then baste.

7. Quilt around outside of all appliquéd pieces. Quilt details on C flowers and leaves, as shown. Quilt center block with quilting design. Fill background with ½ inch crosshatched quilting lines or any simple fill pattern.

8. Bind quilt with medium blue.

c	b	a	b	c
b	c	a	c	b
a	a	plain	a	a
b	c	a	c	b
c	b	a	b	c

Block Assembly Diagram
8 Block a, 8 Block b, 8 Block c
and 1 center plain block

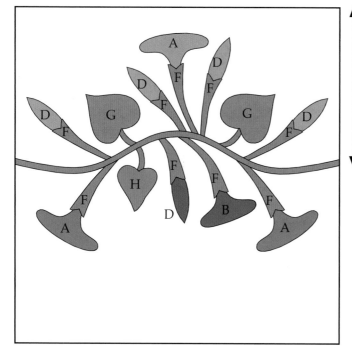

6½"
from vine
to edge of
block

Block a
Make 8 blocks.
Each block contains:
Light blue: 1A flower, 4 D buds
Medium blue: 2 A flowers
Dark blue: 1 B flower, 1 D bud
Green: 9 F calyxes, 2 G leaves, 1 H leaf

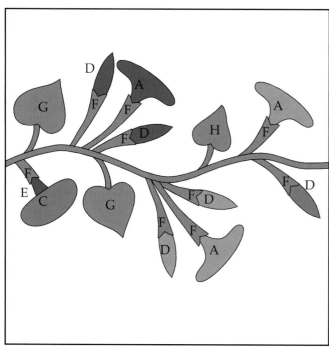

6½"
from vine
to edge of
block

Block b
Make 8 blocks.
Each block contains:
Light blue: 2 A flowers, 2 D buds
Medium blue: 1 C flower, 1 D bud
Dark blue: 1A flower, 2 D buds, 1 E flower base
Green: 9 F calyxes, 2 G leaves, 1 H leaf

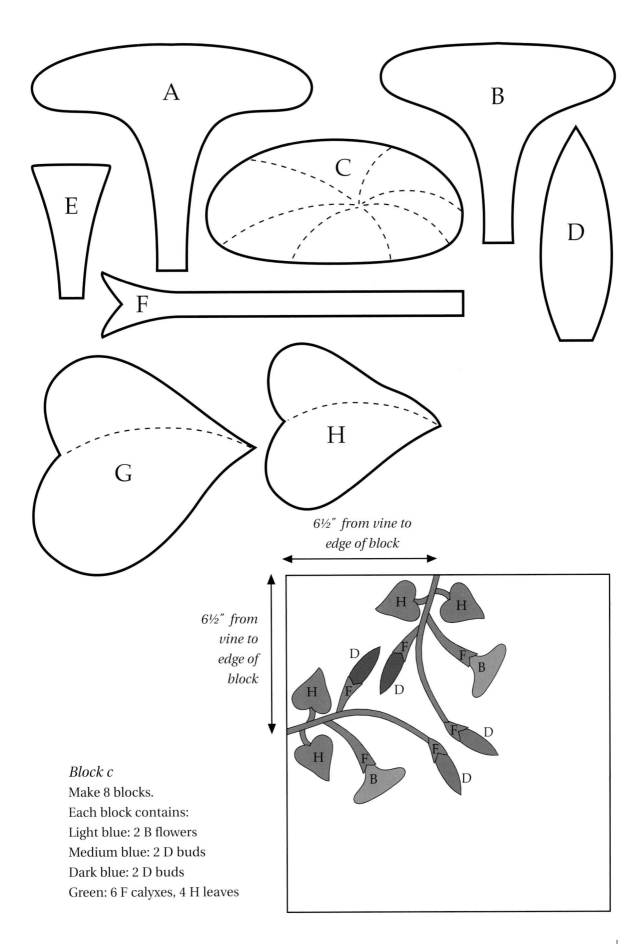

6½″ from vine to edge of block

6½″ from vine to edge of block

Block c
Make 8 blocks.
Each block contains:
Light blue: 2 B flowers
Medium blue: 2 D buds
Dark blue: 2 D buds
Green: 6 F calyxes, 4 H leaves

A

B

C

D

E

F

G

H

Pieced Border Diagram

Border Placement Diagram
Make four borders.
Each border contains:
Light blue: 2 B flowers
Medium blue: 2 D buds
Dark blue: 4 D buds
Green: 8 F calyxes, 5 H leaves

Border Corner Placement Diagram
Make four border corners.
Each border corner contains:
Light blue: 4 B flowers
Medium blue: 4 D buds
Dark blue: 1 B flower, 4 D buds
Green: 13 F calyxes, 8 H leaves

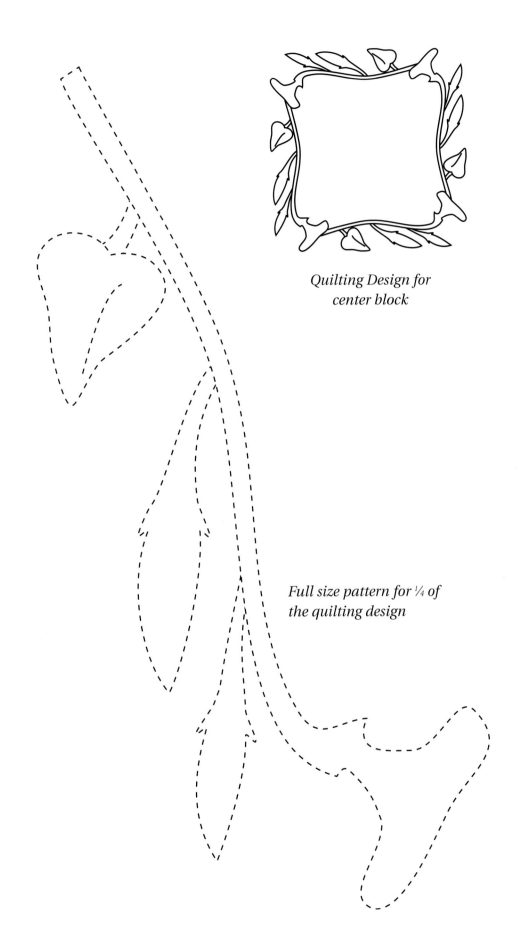

*Quilting Design for
center block*

*Full size pattern for ¼ of
the quilting design*

MORNING GLORY WREATH. 41 x 72 INCHES. COTTON. ALTHOUGH MARIE DESIGNED THE PATTERN IN 1911 OR 1912,
SHE MADE THIS QUILT ABOUT 1940, ONE OF A PAIR SHE GAVE TO HER GRANDDAUGHTERS.
IT IS PROBABLY THE LAST QUILT THAT SHE MADE.
Collection of Rosalind Webster Perry.

Marie Webster's Morning Glory Wreath design was first published in the *Ladies' Home Journal* in August 1912, on a color page with five additional children's quilts of her design. One of these, Butterflies and Pansies, is included in this book. Patterns for Bedtime, Daisy and Sunbonnet Lassies were published in *A Joy Forever*. The sixth baby quilt, Wild Roses, has never been found.

Morning Glory Wreath uses the simplest elements to create an exceptionally graceful design. Only four templates – flower, bud, calyx and leaf – are repeated in clusters to form a large oval wreath, outlined against an unusual two-piece background. The center section is white and the outer section can be made of any favorite pastel color. Marie's first Morning Glory

MORNING GLORY WREATH

Wreath, the one illustrated in the *Ladies' Home Journal*, had a pink outer section. For the quilt shown here – one of a pair she made for her granddaughters about 1940 – green was chosen instead of pink. White and pink flowers are arranged against the green outer background, while pink and blue flowers are appliquéd over the white center. Simple, but very effective!

The construction of this quilt is unusual – one of Marie's innovations. An oval is first carefully measured and cut from the center of the colored background fabric. Then the white center is basted in place to fill the oval. Two intertwined bias strips form the wreath, with the outer curve cleverly concealing the boundary between the two background fabrics. The Vine Templates will help you position the bias strips correctly around the oval.

"It must be 'early to bed and early to rise' for the child who would see the sweet morning glory in all its loveliness, as it must be found before all the dew is gone. Then, too, this delicate flower always curls up and goes to sleep before sunset."

LADIES' HOME JOURNAL, AUGUST 1912

MORNING GLORY WREATH *pattern*

FINISHED SIZES

Quilt: 41″ x 72″
Binding: ¼″ wide

YARDAGE

3 yards light green for leaves, calyxes and background
1¾ yards white for flowers, buds and background
¼ yard pink for flowers and buds
⅛ yard blue for buds
2 yards medium green for leaves, calyxes and vine
2½ yards for backing
½ yard medium green for binding

Light green

Cut 3 yards into 2 pieces:

  2¼ yards and ¾ yard.

Use the full 2¼ yards for background.

After appliqué has been completed,

  trim quilt top to 41½″ x 72½″.

From ¾ yard cut:

  32 C calyxes

Cut calyxes on the bias.

  16 L leaves

For added interest, you may cut

  half of the leaves reversed.

White

1 oval 34½″ x 53″

8 A flowers

20 B buds

Pink

20 A flowers

24 B buds

Blue

8 B buds

Medium green

Cut 2 yards into two 1 yard pieces.

From 1 yard cut:

  48 C calyxes

Cut calyxes on the bias.

  20 L leaves

For added interest, you may cut half of
the leaves reversed.

From 1 yard, cut one continuous bias
strip ¾″ wide for vine.

Backing

Use the 2½ yards for the backing.
If the width of the backing fabric is
less than 45″, you may need to piece
the backing.

Binding

Cut bias strips 1¼″ wide for
¼″ finished single fold binding.

1. Lightly mark an oval 29¼″ x 48″ at the center of the light green background fabric.

Use the Large Vine Template and the Small Vine Template to mark the lines for the bias vine on the green background, referring to the Vine Placement Diagram. Each quarter of the vine consists of five large vine units and one small vine unit. Center the Large Vine Template along the marked line of the oval. Use the Small Vine Template to mark the side centers, where the vine turns in 3½″ from the marked line of the oval.

Note that the vine has an inner curve and an outer curve. Trim away the center of the green fabric, leaving a ¼″ allowance inside the line marked for the outer curve.

2. Center the white background oval under the prepared green background. Pin and baste the two background fabrics together. It is not necessary to turn under the raw edges of the green, as the outer curve of the vine will cover those edges.

The vine will fall partly on the green background and partly on the white background. Using the Vine Templates, mark the vine on the white background, as in step 1.

3. Referring to the Wreath Placement Diagram, cross two bias strips to form the vine on the background fabrics. Take care to place the outer curve of the vine over the raw edges of the green background. Baste in place.

Next position flowers, buds and leaves. Calyxes are placed over flowers and buds. Calyx stems are tucked under the vine and leaves. Place light green leaves and calyxes on white background. Place medium green leaves and calyxes on light green background. Complete appliqué.

4. Layer quilt top, batting and backing, then baste.

5. Quilt around outside of all appliquéd pieces. Fill white center of the wreath with ½″ diamonds. Fill green background with ½″ diagonal quilting lines.

6. Bind quilt with medium green.

Vine Placement Diagram

Wreath Placement Diagram

A=flower, B=bud, C=calyx, L=leaf

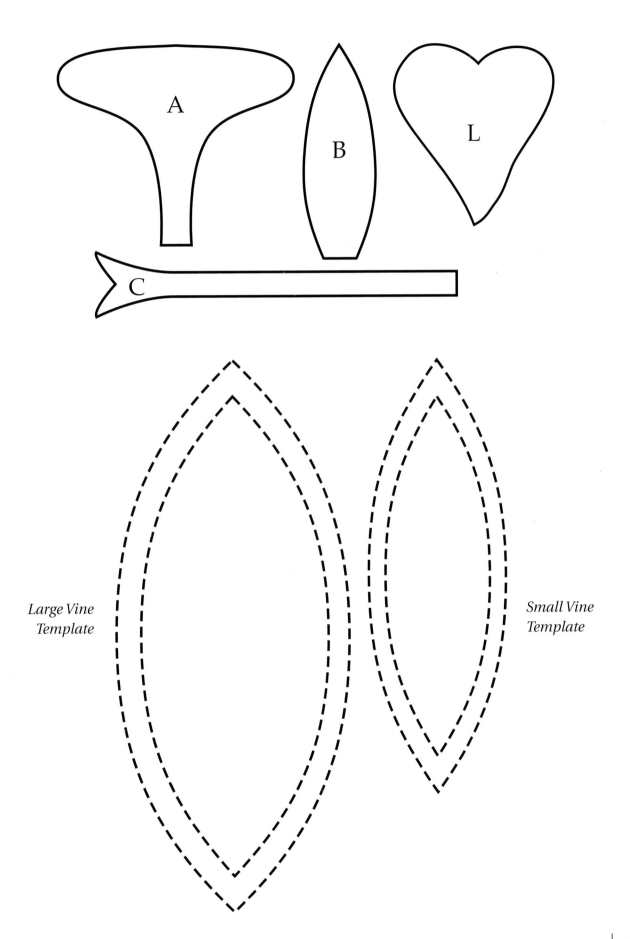

A

B

L

C

Large Vine Template

Small Vine Template

PANSIES AND BUTTERFLIES. 43 x 55 INCHES. LINEN AND COTTON. DESIGNED AND MADE BY MARIE D. WEBSTER.
THIS QUILT IS SIGNED ON THE BACK, "FOR LADIES HOME JOURNAL, 1912. MARIE D. WEBSTER."
Collection of Katherine Webster Dwight.

This delightful baby quilt was pictured in color in the *Ladies' Home Journal* of August 1912, along with Morning Glory Wreath and four other children's quilt designs.

Clouds of butterflies flutter around clusters of pansies, creating a summer garden scene. Each of the 24 butterflies is composed of two overlapping pieces of contrasting shades of yellow. The buds and flowers have yellow and tan petals, but shades of lavender or blue would also work well.

As in many Webster designs, the appliqué is arranged so that the quilt can be viewed from any side without seeming to be "upside down." But don't be fooled! The arrangement of the appliqué is not completely symmetrical, for the bud sometimes appears on the right of the flower cluster, and sometimes on the left.

PANSIES AND BUTTERFLIES

Plain double borders provide a bold, uncluttered frame. In the quilt shown in the *Ladies' Home Journal,* the borders are green rather than yellow.

The quilting incorporates some unusual pointed oval shapes or "lozenges," grouped in the corners, suggesting leaves. The remaining background is simply quilted with Marie's favorite diagonal lines.

Marie Webster's patterns continued to exert a considerable influence decades after they were first published. Both pansies and butterflies became popular design motifs in the 1920s and 1930s, but they were rarely seen together in the same quilt. In 1935, the Nancy Cabot column in the *Chicago Tribune* showed a quilt that is strikingly similar to the Webster design, but without the butterflies.

"As golden butterflies and pansies are so often playmates of little ones in the garden, and beloved by them, they were chosen for the motifs of the pattern....
They will carry happy memories of outdoor play to the bedtime hour."

LADIES' HOME JOURNAL, AUGUST 1912

PANSIES AND BUTTERFLIES *pattern*

FINISHED SIZES

Quilt: 48″ x 60″

Inner rectangle: 30″ x 42″

Yellow Borders: 1½″ wide

White Borders: 6″ wide

Binding: ¼″ wide

YARDAGE

2½ yards white for background and borders

2¼ yards light yellow for borders, pansies
  and butterfly wings

½ yard dark yellow for pansies and butterflies

¼ yard tan for pansies

½ yard green for leaves, calyxes and stems

4 yards for backing

½ yard light yellow for binding

White

Cut 2½ yards into 2 pieces of 1¼ yards.

From one piece, cut center rectangle
   30½″ x 42½″

From second piece cut:
   2 borders 6½″ x 30½″
   2 borders 6½″ x 42½″
   4 corner squares 6½″ x 6½″

Light Yellow

Cut 2¼ yards into 2 pieces:
   1¾ yards and ½ yard.

From 1¾ yard, cut borders:
   Four 2″ x 6½″
   Two 2″ x 30½″
   Two 2″ x 45½″
   Two 2″ x 57½″
   Two 2″ x 60½″

From ½ yard cut:
   8 A petals
   34 F butterfly wings

Dark Yellow

8 B petals and 8 B petals reversed
   for pansies
4 B petals for buds
34 E butterfly bodies

Tan

8 C petals and 8 C petals reversed
   for pansies
4 C petals for buds

Green

4 D calyxes
8 L leaves and 8 L leaves reversed
8 bias strips ¾″ x 6½″ for pansy stems
4 bias strips ¾″ x 2½″ for bud stems

Backing

Cut 4 yards into two 2-yard
pieces. Seam lengthwise.

Binding

Cut bias strips 1¼″ wide for ¼″
finished single fold binding.

1. Referring to the Placement Diagram, complete appliqué on center rectangle. Referring to the full quilt diagram, note the slight differences in the placement of the bud unit and the number of butterflies in each group.

Appliqué bias stems first. Fold bias strips in thirds and stitch down each side. Next appliqué leaves. For pansy, appliqué C petal and C petal reversed first, next appliqué B petal and B petal reversed, then A petal. For bud, appliqué B petal, then C petal and D calyx. For butterfly, appliqué E body and cover with F wings.

2. Complete appliqué of butterflies on border units.

3. Referring to the full quilt diagram, arrange appliquéd center, appliquéd borders and plain border units. Stitch units together.

4. Layer quilt top, batting and backing, then baste.

5. Quilt around outside of all appliquéd pieces. The pointed oval quilting design may be used to create a cable motif, as seen in the photo. Fill remaining areas with diagonal quilting lines.

6. Bind quilt with light yellow.

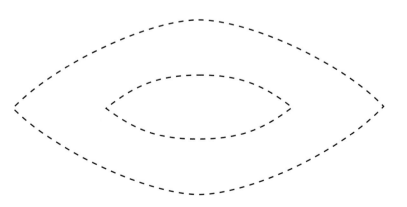

Placement Diagram

A Rose Patchwork Bedroom, *Ladies' Home Journal*, October 1915. This page in the popular magazine featured Marie Webster's Wreath of Roses design for a bedroom ensemble, including a table cover, cushion, dresser scarf, utility bag and chair cover — all decorated with the same motif.
Courtesy of the Indianapolis Museum of Art.

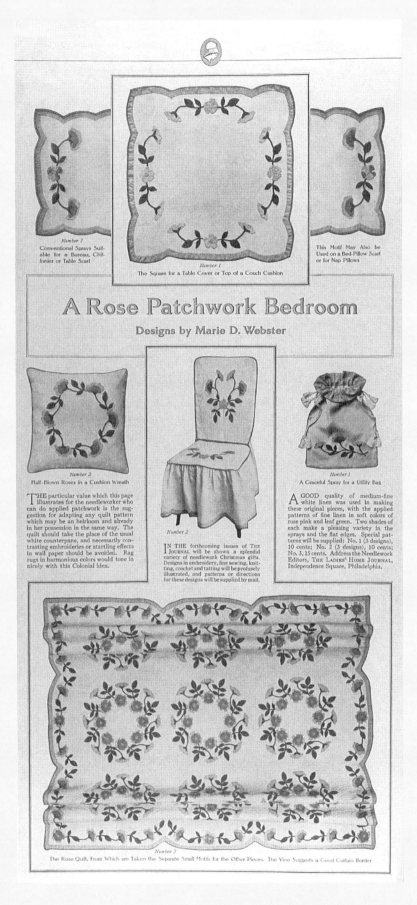

WREATH OF ROSES. 80 x 94 INCHES. COTTON. DESIGNED BY MARIE WEBSTER, 1915.
APPLIQUÉD BY MARIE WEBSTER, 1930. THE NAME OF THE QUILTER IS NOT KNOWN.

Collection of Rosalind Webster Perry.

Wreath of Roses has been one of Marie Webster's most popular patterns ever since its debut in the *Ladies' Home Journal* of October 1915 – the same month in which her landmark book, *Quilts: Their Story and How to Make Them,* was published. Its publisher, Doubleday, Page and Company, vigorously promoted the book, which must have given a boost to Marie's pattern business as well!

Wreath of Roses was just the kind of quilt to appeal to the Colonial Revival sentiment which was sweeping the country. Light and pretty, the design offered a fresh new interpretation of a traditional appliqué favorite. The colors are softly shaded pastels, instead

WREATH OF ROSES

of the brilliant reds and greens of the typical 19th century rose appliqués. The delicately curving outlines of the roses give them a natural, fragile appearance.

The nine blocks are not square, but rectangular, making the whole quilt slightly longer than it is wide. Each wreath is composed of eight flower units and each unit consists of a large rose linked by leaves and bias stems to a smaller rose, which is shown in profile. This arrangement of flowers, stems and leaves creates a circular motion in the blocks, reminiscent of the Wind Blown Tulip pattern. The scalloped border, a popular Colonial Revival treatment, gently echoes the rhythm of the swirling wreaths.

" Full blown roses with rose leaves are arranged in wreaths on each block and a graceful rose vine makes the border. This design is a reminder of quaint, old time quilts and is equally attractive in either pink or yellow for single or double beds. "

"READY TO MAKE QUILTS AND BED SPREADS"
PRACTICAL PATCHWORK COMPANY BROCHURE, ABOUT 1922

WREATH OF ROSES *pattern*

FINISHED SIZES

Quilt: 90″ x 96″

Blocks: 24″ x 26″

White borders: 9″ wide

Pink bias borders: 1¼″ wide

Binding: ¼″ wide

YARDAGE

10 yards white for blocks and borders

1¾ yards light pink for petals

1¼ yards dark pink for petals

¼ yard yellow for centers

2¾ yards green for calyxes, leaves and leaf/stems

1 yard light pink for bias border

9 yards for backing

¾ yard dark pink for binding

White

Cut 10 yards into 2 pieces:
   3 yards and 7 yards.
From 3 yards, cut 2 borders 9½″ x 72½″
   and 2 borders 9½″ x 96½″.
From 7 yards, cut 9 rectangles 24½″ x 26½″.

Light Pink

80 A petals
72 E petals
16 F petals and 16 F petals reversed

Dark Pink

80 B petals
80 C petals
16 G petals and 16 G petals reversed

Yellow

80 D centers

Green

Cut the K calyxes and M leaf/stems on the bias.
104 K calyxes
144 L1 large leaves
240 L2 small leaves
120 M leaf/stems

Pink Bias Border

Cut bias 1¾″ wide for 1¼″ finished border.

Backing

Cut 9 yards into three 3-yard pieces.
Seam lengthwise.

Binding

Cut bias 1¼″ wide for ¼″ finished
single fold binding.

1. Referring to the Block Placement Diagram, complete appliqué on nine rectangular blocks. On each block, arrange eight flower units around a 7-inch circle. First appliqué E petals, then K calyxes. Next appliqué L1 leaves and L2 leaves, then M leaf/stems. Last, appliqué A petals, B petals, C petals and D centers. Sew the 9 appliquéd blocks together.

2. Referring to the Border Placement Diagram, appliqué a flower group at the center of each border. First appliqué L2 leaves, then the 2 M leaf/stems at the ends of the group. Next appliqué F petals and F petals reversed, G petals and G petals reversed, then K calyxes. Next appliqué M leaf/stems near the center. Last, appliqué A petals, B petals, C petals and D centers.

3. Referring to the Border Corner Placement Diagram, appliqué a flower group at each corner. Appliqué units in the same order as for the border, starting with the M leaf/stem at the end and working toward the corner. The appliqué of 1 K calyx and 1 M leaf/stem at each corner will be completed after the borders have been sewn to the blocks.

4. Sew short and long borders to assembled blocks. Complete appliqué at the corners.

5. Appliqué light pink border to white borders. The pink border may be scalloped and the corners rounded, as shown in the quilt diagram.

6. Layer quilt top, batting and backing, then baste.

7. Quilt around all appliquéd pieces. Quilt concentric circles in the center of each wreath and at the block intersections. A rose may be quilted in the center of the circles. Fill remaining areas with single diagonal lines.

8. Bind quilt with dark pink.

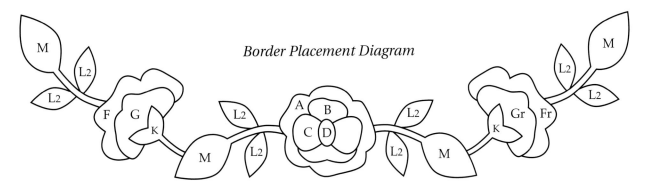

Border Placement Diagram

Block Placement Diagram
One flower unit. Make 8 for
each block.

Border Corner Placement Diagram

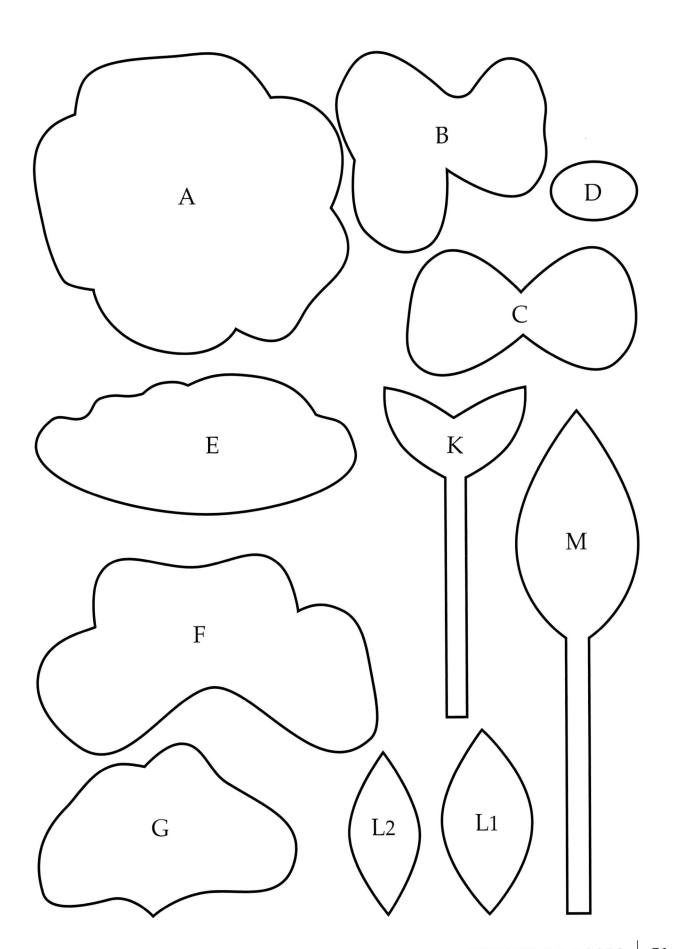

MAGPIE ROSE. 74 X 85½ INCHES. LINEN AND COTTON. DESIGNED AND APPLIQUÉD BY MARIE WEBSTER, ABOUT 1916.
THE NAME OF THE QUILTER IS NOT KNOWN. LIKE MANY OF MARIE'S EARLY QUILTS, THIS BEAUTIFUL QUILT
CONTAINS BOTH LINEN AND COTTON FABRICS.

Indianapolis Museum of Art Webster Collection, Gift of Mrs. Gerrish Thurber.

The name of this quilt is a mystery. Why would a floral quilt be named for a bird? Marie perhaps chose the name because the black-and-white striped fabric in the baskets and border reminded her of the magpie, a large bird with a bold black and white pattern.

This quilt was heavily used by the family, and faded from repeated washings. Marie later covered several stains with new buds, which retain their fresh colors. Nevertheless, this is a lovely quilt, with exquisite quilting. A large oval wreath of flowers fills the middle of the quilt, with a basket of roses in each corner. Tiny rose petals, barely visible because of the fading, are strewn across the center of the oval, which is quilted with a rose design.

The technique of reverse appliqué was used for both large and small roses. In the small roses, the dark pink rose center C is placed beneath the medium pink rose B, so that

MAGPIE ROSE

it shows through the hole cut out of the center of the upper piece. The 14 large roses in the oval have an additional light pink piece A as a base. Similar reverse appliquéd roses also appear in the Cluster of Roses and Dutch Basket patterns.

To make the flowers look more natural, Marie introduced random variations in the placement of the petals, buds and flowers. You may vary the orientation of the flowers in each block, as well as the placement of the buds in each bud unit. The lighter colored bud may be placed above or below the darker bud, to its right or to its left. The Block and Border Placement Diagrams show a suggestion for the bud placement. The loose petals should be scattered randomly. Some may be reversed for added interest.

A variation of this pattern substitutes green for the black-and-white fabric of the baskets and border, as in Ruth Levy's Magpie Rose quilt illustrated on page 25.

"In this quilt pink roses are arranged in a graceful oval wreath in whose center rose petals are strewn.... Along the border of black and white a rose vine with its opening buds is festooned in graceful curves."

"THE NEW PATCHWORK QUILT PATTERNS"
MARIE WEBSTER'S BROCHURE

MAGPIE ROSE *pattern*

Quilt: 77½″ x 88½″

Blocks:

 6 blocks 21½″ x 21½″

 3 blocks 21½″ x 32½″

Borders: 6½″ wide

 (includes 3″ striped

 border and ½″ vine)

Binding: ¼″ wide

9 yards white for blocks and borders

1½ yards light pink for roses, petals and buds

½ yard medium pink for roses

¾ yard dark pink for rose centers and buds

2 yards black-and-white striped fabric for baskets and borders

 Note: Stripes should run lengthwise.

3 yards green for leaves, calyxes, stems and vine

6 yards for backing

½ yard black-and-white stripe for binding

White

Cut 9 yards into 2 pieces: 6 yards and 3 yards.

From 6 yards, cut 6 squares 22″ x 22″
and 3 rectangles 22″ x 33″.

From 3 yards, cut 2 borders 7″ x 78″
and 2 borders 7″ x 89″.

Light pink

14 A roses

72 D buds

14 E petals

30 F petals

Medium pink

22 B roses

Dark pink

22 C rose centers

72 D buds

Black-and-white stripe

Cut 2 yards into 3 pieces: ½ yard, ½ yard and 1 yard.

From ½ yard, cut 4 G baskets.

From ½ yard, cut 1″ bias strips for handles.

From 1 yard, cut ten strips 3½″ x width of fabric.

Seam 2 strips for each short border. Trim to 3½″ x 78″.

Seam 3 strips for each long border. Trim to 3½″ x 89″.

Green

Cut 3 yards into 3 pieces: 1¾ yd, ½ yd and ¾ yd.

From 1¾ yard cut:

 72 K calyxes

 6 L1 leaves

 112 L2 leaves

 4 M1 leaf/stems and 4 M1 leaf/stems reversed

 26 M2 leaf/stems and 22 M2 leaf/stems reversed

Note: Cut M1 and M2 leaf/stems on the bias.

From ½ yard, cut ¾″ wide bias strips for stems.

From ¾ yard, cut 1″ wide bias strips for vine.

Backing

Cut 6 yards into two 3-yard pieces. Seam lengthwise.

Binding

This quilt has straight grain binding.

Cut ten strips 1¼″ wide x width of the striped fabric. Seam two strips for each short border. Seam three strips for each long border.

1. Referring to the Block Placement Diagrams, complete appliqué on 9 blocks. To prepare B roses for reverse appliqué, trim away centers, leaving ¼″ turn-under allowance from the turn line. Clip to the turn line at the inner corners. Baste C rose centers under B roses.

 Make 4 Block a. Appliqué basket handles first and then bias stems, G baskets, L2 small leaves, M2 small leaf/stems and M2 small leaf/stems reversed, D buds and K calyxes. Appliqué small roses. Appliqué a bud unit (one light pink D bud, one dark pink D bud and one K calyx) in each corner.

 Make 2 Block b. Appliqué bias stems first, then L1 large leaves, L2 small leaves, M1 large leaf/stems and M1 large leaf/stems reversed. Appliqué large roses. Appliqué a bud unit in each corner. Appliqué E and F petals.

 Make 2 Block c. Appliqué bias stems first, then L1 large leaves, L2 small leaves, M1 large leaf/stems, M1 large leaf/stems reversed, M2 small leaf/stems and M2 small leaf/stems reversed. Appliqué bud units, large roses and small roses. Appliqué F petals.

 Make one Block d. Appliqué E and F petals, then appliqué a bud unit in each corner.

2. Referring to the Border Placement Diagram, complete appliqué on borders.

 Mark a scalloped edge along the long side of the black-and-white border. Trim ¼″ from marked line. Baste black-and-white border to white border, matching the outside raw edges.

 Appliqué bias stems, then L2 small leaves, M2 small leaf/stems and M2 small leaf/stems reversed, D buds and K calyxes. Appliqué green vine along the scalloped edge, covering the ends of the stems and the raw edge of the black-and-white border.

3. Referring to the full quilt diagram, stitch together the 9 appliquéd blocks. Add appliquéd borders, mitering corner seams.

4. Layer quilt top, batting and backing, then baste.

5. Quilt around outside of all appliquéd pieces. Center may be quilted with roses and small diamonds. Use any preferred quilting designs for the remaining areas.

6. Bind quilt with black-and-white stripe, matching the stripes of the border.

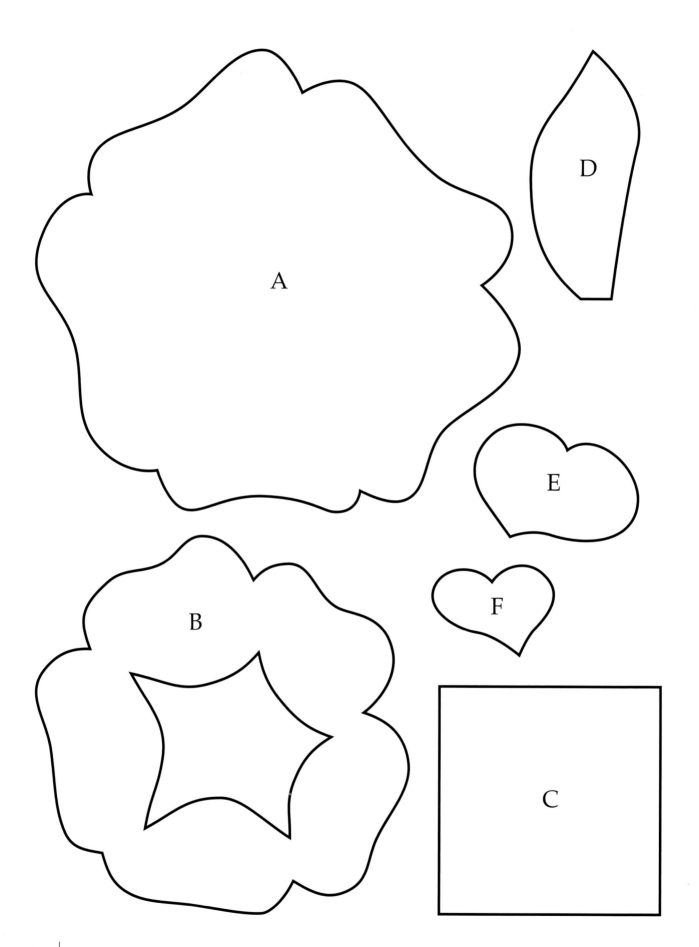

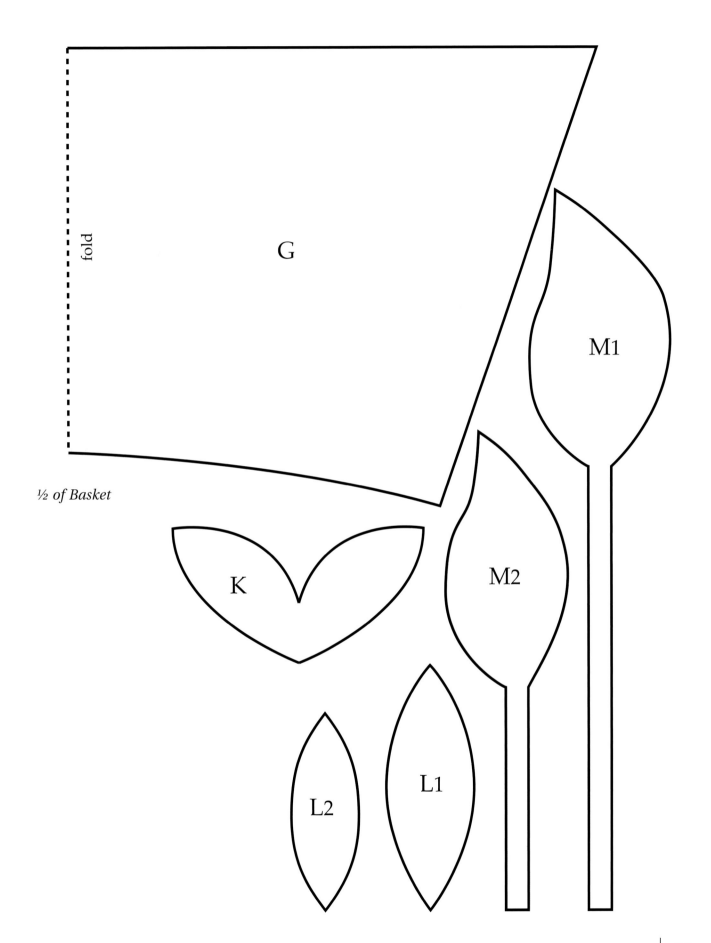

fold

G

½ of Basket

K

M1

M2

L1

L2

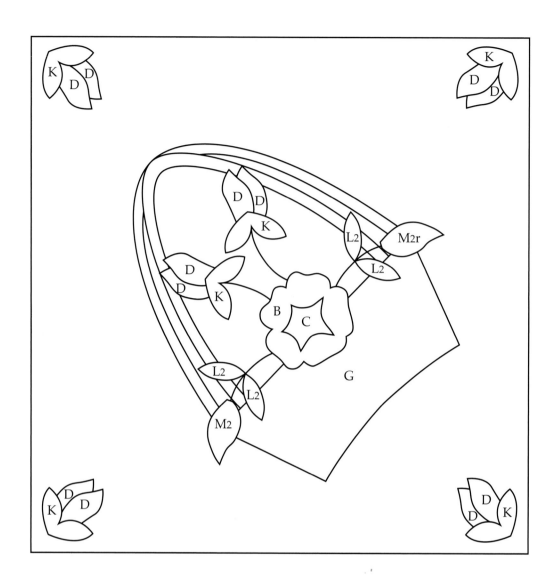

Placement Diagram for Block a

Placement Diagram for Block b

Border Placement Diagram

Placement Diagram for Block c

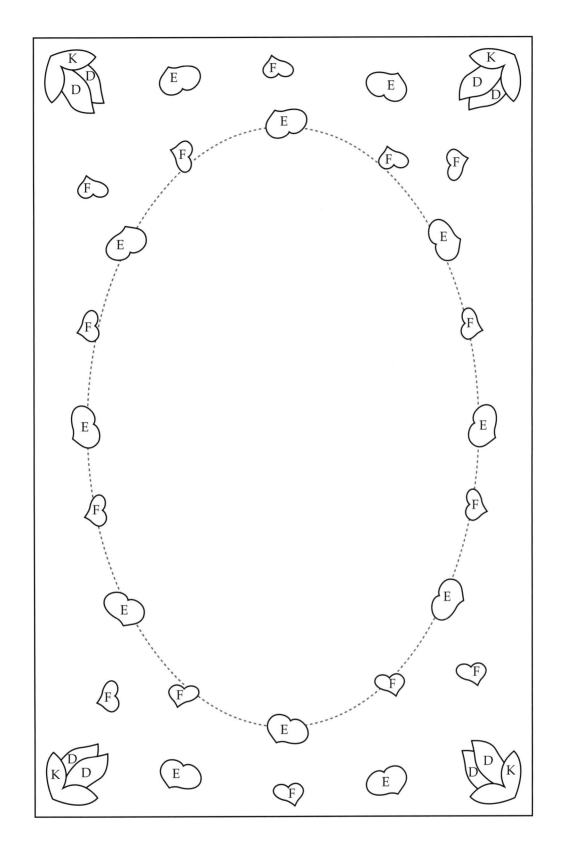

Placement Diagram for Block d

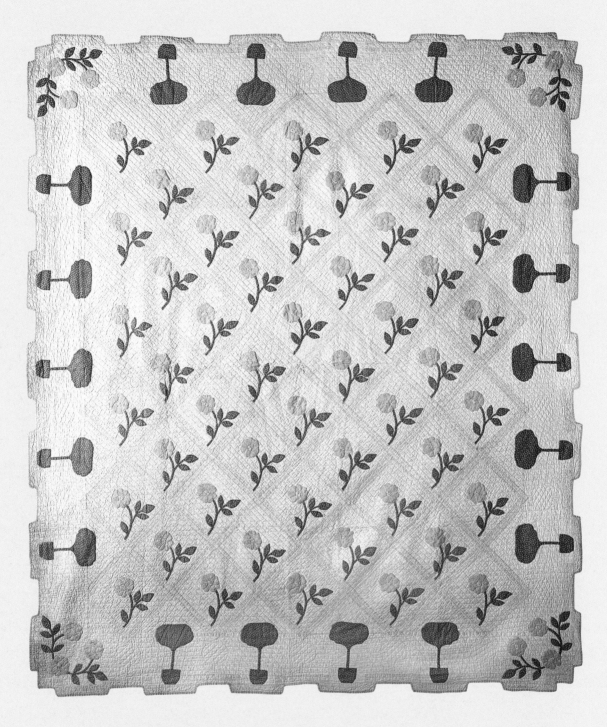

CHEROKEE ROSE. 73 x 83 INCHES. COTTON. DESIGNED AND APPLIQUÉD BY MARIE WEBSTER, ABOUT 1916.
THE NAME OF THE QUILTER IS NOT KNOWN. THIS WELL-LOVED AND MUCH-USED QUILT WAS
FEATURED IN *NEEDLECRAFT* MAGAZINE, SEPT. 1930.
Collection of Katherine Webster Dwight.

The Cherokee rose is the state flower of Georgia and was said to be a special favorite of the Cherokee Indians. The old-fashioned simplicity of this wild rambling rose evokes the colonial era; in the 1920s, Cherokee roses were planted in the gardens of Colonial Williamsburg.

Although Marie started her Cherokee Rose quilt in 1916, it was not widely known until 1930, when it was published in *Needlecraft* magazine. Its popularity grew when Ruby McKim included a variation of the Webster design in her famous state flower quilt pattern in 1931.

The three quilts which Marie made in 1916 and 1917 – Magpie Rose, Cherokee Rose and Poinsettia – were her only full-size quilts using printed fabrics. In Cherokee Rose, she chose a yellow print for the rose centers and a green print for the leaves and trees.

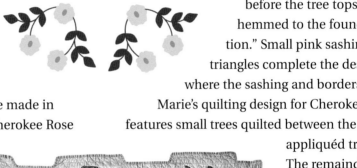

CHEROKEE ROSE

The blocks are set on point to give the quilt a dynamic quality. But it is in the border that Marie's originality is most striking. As she said in her *Needlecraft* article, "Many will consider the border of this really beautiful quilt its distinctive feature, noting the quaint little potted trees, primly upstanding, each in its own space.... It will be seen that the upper part of each little tree rests on a triangular block at the edge of the quilt itself; hence the border must be added before the tree tops are hemmed to the foundation." Small pink sashing triangles complete the design, where the sashing and borders meet. Marie's quilting design for Cherokee Rose features small trees quilted between the appliquéd trees. The remainder is quilted with hanging diamonds – horizontal lines one-half inch apart crossed by diagonal lines at one-inch intervals.

"It may be said without fear of contradiction that in all the categories of old-time quilts there is scarcely one to compare with the 'Cherokee Rose,' as famous in days gone by as in the present renaissance of the quiltmaker's art."

NEEDLECRAFT MAGAZINE, SEPTEMBER 1930

CHEROKEE ROSE *pattern*

FINISHED SIZES

Quilt: 79⅝″ x 92⅜″

Blocks: 8″ x 8″

Sashing: 1″ wide

White Borders:
    8″ wide
    (includes 1″ wide pink bars)

Binding: ¼″ wide

YARDAGE

7½ yards white for borders, blocks and triangles

⅛ yard yellow for rose centers

1 yard dark pink for petals

3 yards light pink for sashing, sashing triangles
    and bars

2 yards green for stems, leaves, trees and pots

6 yards for backing

¾ yard dark pink for binding

White

Cut 7½" yards of white into 2 pieces:
    4½ yards and 3 yards.
From 4½ yards cut:
    50 background squares 8½" x 8½"
    5 squares 12⅝" x 12⅝". Cut diagonally in
      both directions to make 18 side triangles.
    2 squares 6⅝" x 6⅝". Cut diagonally to
      make 4 corner triangles.
From 3 yards cut:
    2 borders 8½" x 92⅞"
    2 borders 8½" x 80⅛"

Yellow

62 D rose centers

Dark Pink

62 A petals, 62 B petals, 62 C petals

Light Pink

60 sashing strips 1½" x 8½"
2 sashing strips 1½" x 10½"
2 sashing strips 1½" x 28½"
2 sashing strips 1½" x 46½"
2 sashing strips 1½" x 64½"
2 sashing strips 1½" x 82½"
1 sashing strip   1½" x 91½"
11 squares 1⅞" x 1⅞". Cut diagonally to make
    22 sashing triangles.
56 bars 1½" x 8½" for border

Green

Cut 2 yards into 2 pieces: 1½ yards and ½ yard.
From 1½ yards cut:
    182 L leaves
    58 M leaf/stems
    Cut M leaf/stems on the bias.
From ½ yard, cut 58 bias stems ¾" wide x 8".

Backing

Cut 6 yards into two 3-yard pieces.
Seam lengthwise.

Binding

Cut bias strips 1¼" wide for ¼" finished
single fold binding.

1. Referring to the Block Placement Diagram, complete appliqué on fifty blocks. Appliqué M leaf/stem first, then L leaves and stems. Next appliqué A, B and C petals, then D center.

2. Referring to the Border Placement Diagram, complete appliqué on 4 borders, except for T trees and the corner roses. These will be appliquéd after the borders have been added to the blocks.

    Position trees so that they will be centered on each side triangle. Appliqué E trunks and P pots. The T trees cover the seam. Partially baste T trees in place.

    Center a bar under each tree and in between the trees. The bars overlap 1⅝". Bars at the corners will be shortened when caught in the mitered seam.

    At the corners, appliqué M leaf/stems, then L leaves and stems. Next appliqué A, B, and C petals and D centers. The M leaf/stems may overlap the bars.

3. Referring to the full quilt diagram, assemble the appliquéd blocks with the background triangles and sashing. Sew the units into diagonal rows. Sew the rows together.

4. Add appliquéd borders, mitering the corner seams. Complete appliqué of trees and corner roses. Appliqué light pink triangles where the sashing meets the borders.

5. Layer quilt top, batting and backing, then baste.

6. Quilt around outside of all appliquéd pieces. Fill remaining areas with small diamonds.

7. Bind quilt with dark pink.

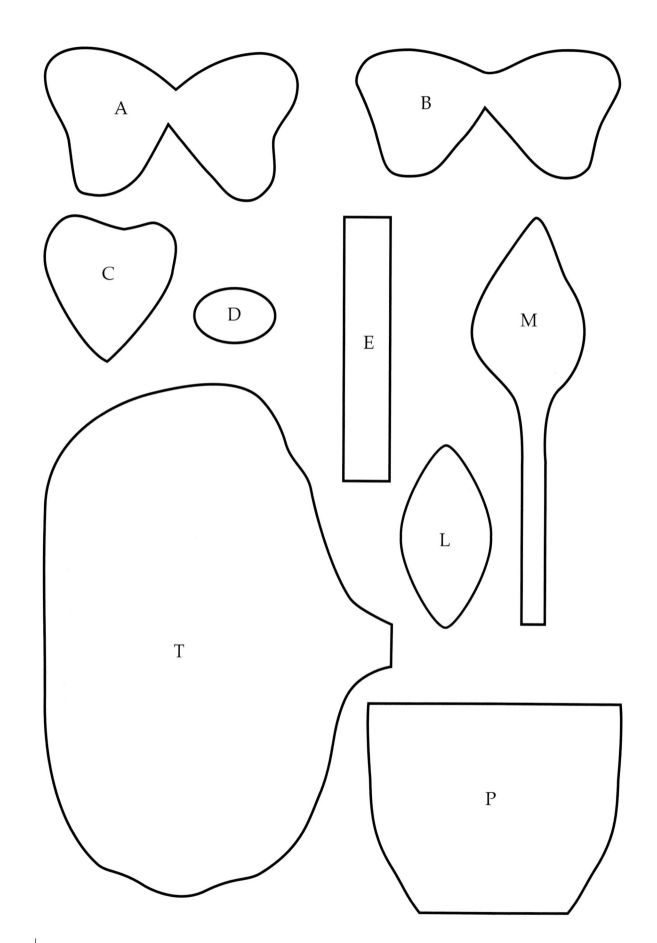

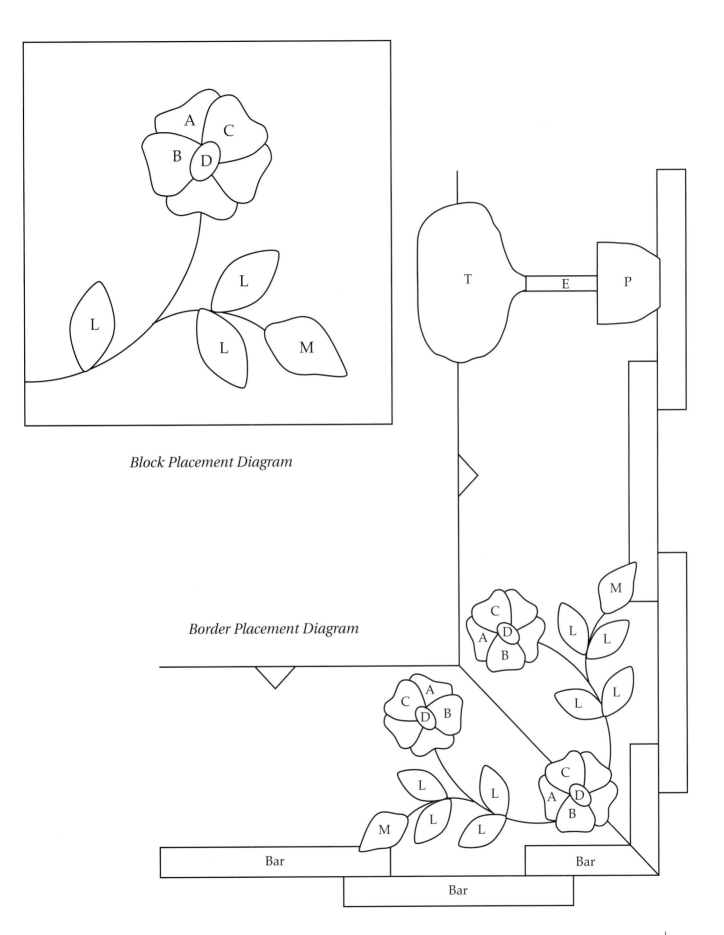

Block Placement Diagram

Border Placement Diagram

CLUSTER OF ROSES. 77 X 90 INCHES. COTTON. THIS LIGHT AND GRACEFUL QUILT WAS APPLIQUÉD IN 1930 BY MARIE WEBSTER'S
SISTER, EMMA DAUGHERTY, FROM THE PATTERN DESIGNED BY MARIE ABOUT 1922. THE NAME OF THE QUILTER IS NOT KNOWN.
EMMA WORKED ALONGSIDE MARIE IN HER QUILT PATTERN BUSINESS AND WAS ALSO A PROFICIENT NEEDLEWOMAN.
Collection of Mrs. H. Edward Rietze III.

Marie designed this elegant pattern in the early 1920s. It was first mentioned in a 1922 article about the Practical Patchwork Company which appeared in the *Marion Daily Chronicle*. Marie and her friends, Evangeline Beshore and Ida Hess, sold kits and quilts in many of the Webster patterns. Cluster of Roses was included in their little illustrated catalog of "Quilts and Spreads" as a kit "stamped on white or color," as a basted quilt top, or even as a completely finished quilt. They also sold kits for a Cluster of Roses bedspread, with the flowers arranged in an overall design, rather than on nine blocks.

The early 1920s marked a distinct change in Marie's designs. Most of her new quilt patterns featured simple shapes and repeated blocks, so they would be easier to package as kits. They would also be easier for the customer

CLUSTER OF ROSES

to appliqué, giving them wider appeal.

The roses in this quilt resemble the ones in Magpie Rose and Dutch Basket, which also use the technique of reverse appliqué. Each flower has a dark pink center which shows through a hole cut in the light pink rose.

In spite of the simple shapes, the interplay of buds and leaves across the block boundaries creates a lively secondary design. Note that the blocks are rectangular rather than square.

The batting is very thin cotton, making this an exceptionally delicate and lightweight quilt. The anonymous quilter has done a fine job with lovely feathered wreaths between the rose clusters. The background quilting consists of diagonals, while the center of each cluster is accented by diamonds. The light pink bias border, which has not been quilted, is gently scalloped.

" This – the fifth member of the ever popular 'Rose' Family – is a most worthy companion for her beautiful older sisters [American Beauty Rose, Wreath of Roses, Magpie Rose and Cherokee Rose]. Clusters of full blooming roses, interwoven with the fresh green of their own leaves, are placed in the center of each of the nine blocks. "

"THE NEW PATCHWORK QUILT PATTERNS"
MARIE WEBSTER'S BROCHURE

CLUSTER OF ROSES *pattern*

FINISHED SIZES

Quilt: 90″ x 96″

Blocks: 24″ x 26″

White borders: 9″ wide

Pink bias borders: 1¼″ wide

Binding: ¼″ wide

YARDAGE

10 yards white for blocks and borders

1½ yards light pink for roses

1 yard light pink for bias border

1 yard dark pink for roses and buds

3¼ yards green for leaves and calyxes

9 yards for backing

¾ yard dark pink for binding

White
Cut 10 yards into 2 pieces:
  3 yards and 7 yards.
From 3 yards cut:
  2 borders 9½″ x 72½″
  2 borders 9½″ x 96½″
From 7 yards, cut 9 rectangles
  24½″ x 26½″

Light Pink
36 A roses
36 B roses

Dark Pink
36 C1 rose centers
36 C2 rose centers
80 D buds

Green
*Cut the calyxes and leaf/stems
  on the bias.*
80 K calyxes
192 L1 leaves
192 L2 leaves
96 M leaf/stems

Light Pink Bias Border
Cut 1¾″ wide bias for 1¼″
finished border.

Backing
Cut 9 yards into three 3-yard pieces.
Seam together lengthwise.

Binding
Cut bias 1¼″ wide for ¼″ finished
single fold binding.

1. To prepare A and B roses for reverse appliqué, trim away centers, leaving ¼″ turn-under allowance from the turn line. Clip to the turn line at the inner corners. Baste C1 rose center under A rose. Baste C2 rose center under B rose.

2. Referring to the Block Placement Diagram, complete appliqué on nine blocks. Appliqué D buds first, then K calyxes. Appliqué M leaf/stems, covering ends of calyxes. Appliqué L1 and L2 leaves. Reverse appliqué A roses over C1 centers.

3. Sew the nine blocks together.

4. Referring to the Border Placement Diagram, partially complete appliqué on the borders. Some of the roses cover the seams and will be appliquéd after the borders have been added to the blocks. Center a border rose group on each block seam. Appliqué M leaf/stems, L1 leaves and L2 leaves. Reverse appliqué B roses over C2 centers.

5. Referring to the Corner Placement Diagram, partially complete appliqué at border corners. One rose, 1 bud and 1 calyx in each corner will be appliquéd after the borders have been added to the blocks. Appliqué M leaf/stems, L1 leaves and L2 leaves. Appliqué D buds and K calyxes. Reverse appliqué B roses over C2 centers.

6. Sew borders to blocks. Complete appliqué on borders.

7. Appliqué light pink bias to outside edge of white borders. The bias may be tapered as shown in the diagram to give the quilt a scalloped edge.

8. Layer quilt top, batting and back, then baste.

9. Quilt around all appliquéd pieces. A feathered wreath may be appliquéd where the blocks meet. Fill remaining areas with diagonal lines. Note that the light pink bias border is not quilted.

10. Bind edges with dark pink.

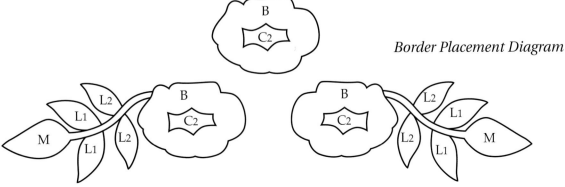

Border Placement Diagram

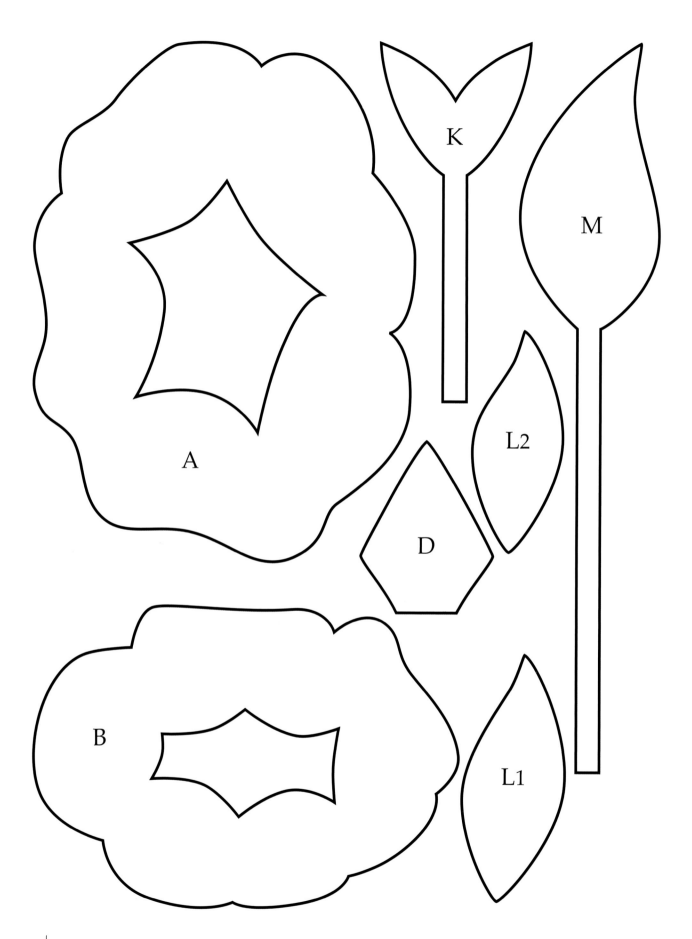

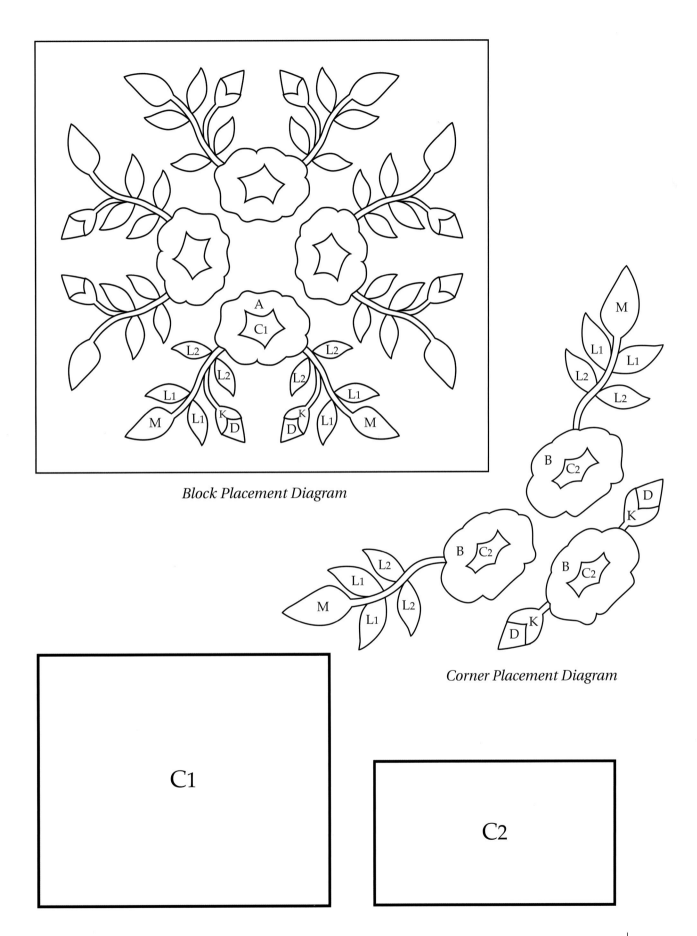

Block Placement Diagram

Corner Placement Diagram

C1

C2

DUTCH BASKET. 75 x 90 INCHES. COTTON. HAND APPLIQUÉD AND HAND PIECED ABOUT 1930
BY GRACE MUELLER DENMAN OF DANVILLE, ILLINOIS.

*Collection of Mrs. John E. Sebat. Photo courtesy of the Illinois Quilt Research Project, Land of Lincoln
Quilters Association and the Early American Museum, Mahomet, Illinois.*

This design, dating from about 1922, marks Marie's first experiment with multi-colored appliqué – a bright palette of solid color cottons – in contrast to the more restrained color combinations of her earlier quilts.

Not only did she try new color combinations, she also introduced a variety of different flowers. According to her catalog, "This new design has quaint blue baskets filled with pink and yellow tulips... connected with garlands of pink roses and lavender morning glories." It has a definite folk quality, with simple, clearly defined shapes in a highly stylized design – perfect for a Colonial Revival decorating scheme.

Reverse appliqué is extensively used in this pattern – for the large center baskets, the smaller border baskets and for both the large and small roses. A variation of this design was sold as a bedspread kit, either stamped, basted, or completely finished. The border treatment of the spread omits the scalloped edge and small baskets. Instead, tulips and morning glories are clustered along a straight border, outlined with colored stripes.

The Dutch Basket pattern is rarely seen, but has always been one of my favorites, because a pair of these bedspreads was in daily use in our home when I was a small child. The design was appliquéd onto a single layer of heavy muslin, so that every one of my grandmother's appliqué stitches was visible on the back. Those stitches were remarkably tiny, even and neat!

DUTCH BASKET

"These quilts are treasures that were intended to be a part of life and art. Her designs are a delight in color and celebrations of nature in its truest sense."

NILOO IMAMI-PAYDAR, *AMERICAN QUILT RENAISSANCE,* 1997

DUTCH BASKET *pattern*

FINISHED SIZES

Quilt: 72″ x 96″
Blocks: 24″ x 36″
Borders: 12″ wide
Binding: ¼″ wide

YARDAGE

10½ yards white for background and borders
¾ yard light pink for roses and tulips
¼ yard medium pink for rose centers
1 yard blue for baskets
½ yard lavender for morning glories and tulips
½ yard yellow for tulips
1½ yards green for leaves and stems
6 yards for backing
1 yard blue for binding

White

Cut 10½ yards into 2 pieces:
    6 yards and 4½ yards.
From 4½ yards cut:
    4 rectangles 24½″ x 36½″
From 6 yards cut:
    2 borders 12½″ x 72½″
    2 borders 12½″ x 96½″

Light Pink

4 A roses
16 B roses
8 F tulips

Medium Pink

20 C rose centers

Lavender

32 D morning glories
8 F tulips

Blue

4 G1 baskets
4 G2 baskets

Yellow

16 E tulips
8 F tulips

Green

Cut 1½ yards into 2 pieces:
    1 yard and ½ yard.
From 1 yard cut:
    24 L1 leaves
    48 L2 leaves
    16 M leaf/stems
From ½ yard, cut bias strips
¾″ wide for stems and vines.

Backing

Cut 6 yards into two 3-yard pieces.
Seam lengthwise.

Binding

Cut bias strips 1¼″ wide for ¼″
finished single fold binding.

1. To prepare A and B roses for reverse appliqué, trim away centers, leaving ¼″ turn-under allowance from the turn line. Clip to the turn line at the inner corners. Baste C rose centers under A and B.

To prepare G1 and G2 baskets for reverse appliqué, trim away center of oval and triangle areas, leaving ¼″ turn-under allowance from the turn line. Clip triangle areas to the inner corners.

2. Referring to the Block Placement Diagram, complete appliqué on four blocks. Each basket contains 3 tulips and 2 leaves. Appliqué center yellow F tulip first, then L2 leaves. Last, appliqué a pink F tulip and a lavender F tulip on either side of the leaves.

Pin G1 basket in place. Appliqué the vine, running the vine over and under the basket handle. Appliqué G1 basket.

Appliqué L1 leaves, M leaf/stems and L2 leaves. Appliqué D morning glories, then stems, covering the ends of the morning glories with the stems. Appliqué E tulips. Reverse appliqué B roses over C centers. Appliqué of large A roses will be completed after the blocks are sewn together.

3. Referring to the Border Placement Diagram, complete appliqué on borders. Each basket contains 3 tulips and 2 leaves. Appliqué center yellow F tulip first, then L2 leaves. Next, appliqué a pink F tulip and a lavender F tulip on either side of the leaves.

Pin G2 basket in place. Baste the vine in place, running the vine over and under the basket handle. Appliqué G2 basket.

Appliqué L1 leaves, tucking ends under the vine. Next appliqué M leaf/stems and L2 leaves. Appliqué D morning glories, then stems. Cover the end of each morning glory with the stem and tuck end of stem under the vine. Appliqué the vine.

Appliqué E tulips. Reverse appliqué B roses over C centers.

4. Stitch the four appliquéd blocks together. Appliqué A roses over C centers. Add borders, mitering the corner seams. The outer edges may be scalloped or left straight.

5. Layer quilt top, batting and backing, then baste.

6. Quilt around outside of all appliquéd pieces. Fill remaining areas with feathered plumes and diamonds.

7. Bind quilt with blue.

Block Placement Diagram

Border Placement Diagram

A

E

F

C

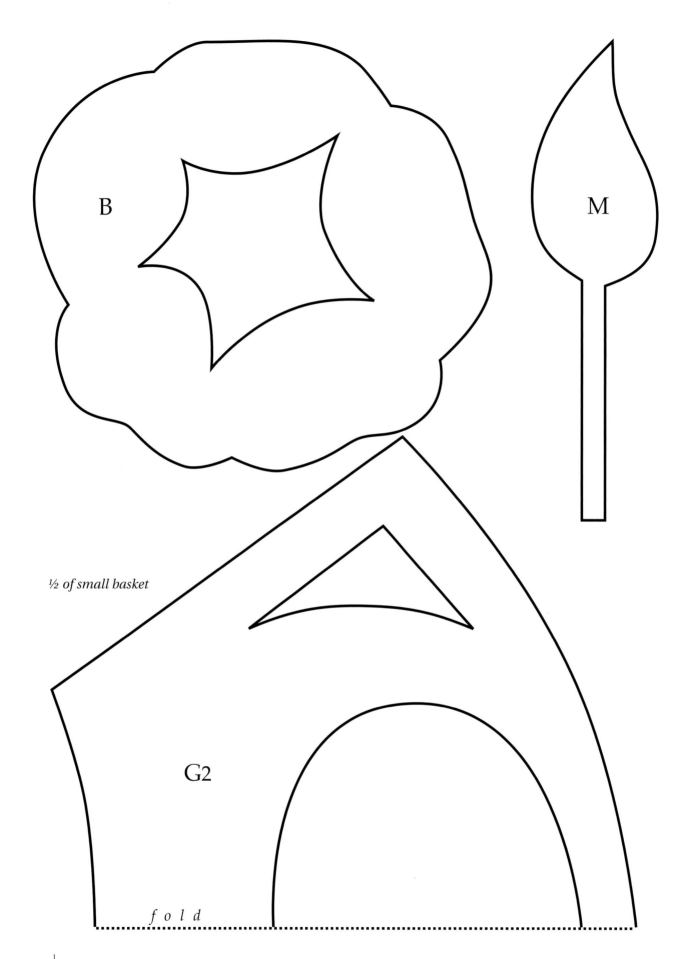

B

M

½ *of small basket*

G2

f o l d

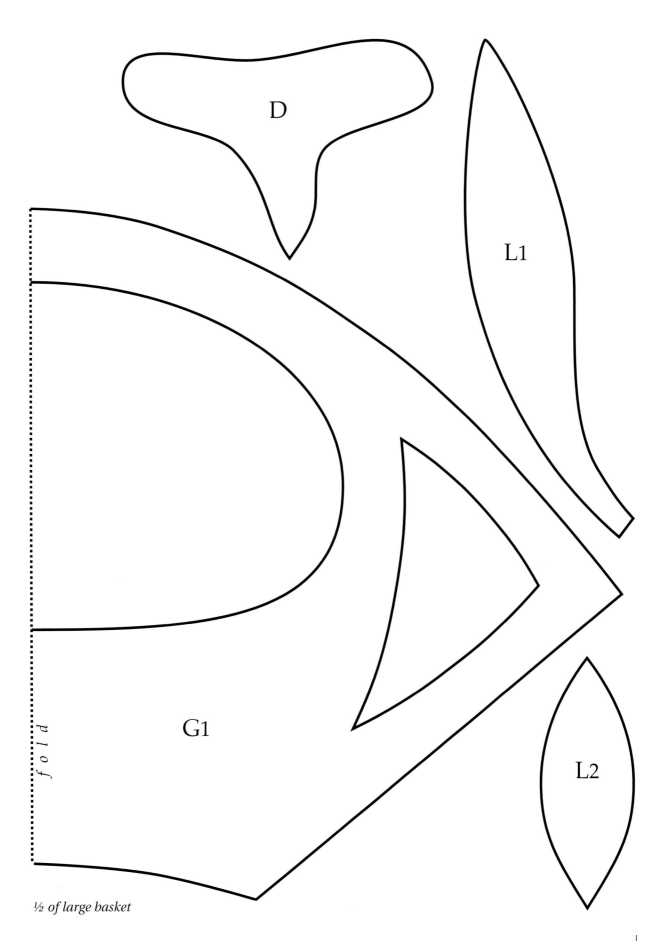

D

L1

L2

G1

f o l d

½ *of large basket*

PRIMROSE WREATH. 68½ x 95 INCHES. COTTON. DESIGNED BY MARIE WEBSTER.
THE BACK IS INSCRIBED: "PRIMROSE WREATH, 1925." IT IS NOT KNOWN IF SHE APPLIQUÉD THE QUILT,
WHICH WAS PART OF HER PERSONAL COLLECTION.
Indianapolis Museum of Art Webster Collection, Gift of Mrs. Gerrish Thurber.

A perennial favorite, Primrose Wreath was designed for the kit market in the mid-1920s. The quilt could be ordered from the Practical Patchwork Company, stamped on a white background for $10, stamped on a colored background for $12, basted for $30, or as a completely finished quilt for $70. The fabrics were Peter Pan, "a closely woven, light weight fabric with a soft dull finish. Its soft texture makes it a joy with which to work, and it takes the needle readily...." It is "the quilt makers ideal material... the very best obtainable for quilt making," according to Marie's contemporary, quilt shop owner Mary McElwain, who sold many Webster kits and patterns in her famous shop in Walworth, Wisconsin.

Each large wreath is composed of six stylized primroses, designed to be easy to appliqué. The border is especially charming, with

PRIMROSE WREATH

its row of jaunty little flowers – very much in the Art Deco style. Note the alternating deep and shallow scallops along the edge of the quilt, with an extra primrose tucked into the exaggerated, rounded corners. The centers of the flower wreaths have been quilted with beautiful feathered wreaths.

The quilt illustrated here features a variety of solid colors – green, dark and light blue, dark and light lavender, and dark, medium and light peach. However, the flowers in the original Practical Patchwork kits were either all pink or all blue.

The Primrose Wreath pattern was published in *Lady's Circle Patchwork Quilts* in its Winter 1988 Editor's Choice issue, proving the continued appeal of this classic design. According to the magazine, "This lovely quilt is certainly 'easy appliqué,' with its simple vines trailing around [the] blocks.... The elaborate quilting turns a beginner appliqué into a masterpiece quilt!"

"The quilt is such a lovely bed covering that the possessor of one of pleasing design and harmonious colors never glances at it without justifiable pride."

"QUILTS AND SPREADS"
MARIE WEBSTER'S BROCHURE

PRIMROSE WREATH *pattern*

FINISHED SIZES

Quilt: 72″ x 90″

Blocks: 18″ x 18″

Border: 9″ wide

Binding: ¼″ wide

YARDAGE

6½ yards white for blocks and borders

½ yard light peach for block flowers

½ yard medium peach for border flowers and block flower centers

½ yard dark peach for border flower centers and buds

½ yard light blue for block flowers

⅛ yard dark blue for block flower centers

½ yard light lavender for block flowers

⅛ yard dark lavender for block flower centers

2 yards green for leaves and stems

6 yards for backing

¾ yard dark peach for binding

White

Cut 6½ yards into 2 pieces:
   3 yards and 3½ yards.
From 3 yards, cut
   2 borders 9½″ x 72½″
   2 borders 9½″ x 90½″
From 3½ yards, cut
   12 blocks 18½″ x 18½″

Light peach

96 A petals

Medium peach

72 A petals
24 C centers

Dark peach

36 A petals
18 C centers

Light blue

96 A petals

Dark blue

24 C centers

Light lavender

96 A petals

Dark lavender

24 C centers

Green

Cut 2 yards into 2 pieces:
   1¼ yards and ¾ yards.
From 1¼ yards cut:
   36 L1 leaves
   180 L2 leaves
   36 B bud stems
From ¾ yard, cut ¾″ wide bias for stems.

Backing

Cut 6 yards into two 3-yard pieces.
Seam lengthwise.

Binding

Cut bias strips 1¼″ wide for ¼″
finished single fold binding.

1. Referring to the Block Placement Diagram, complete appliqué on 12 blocks. Each block contains 2 peach, 2 blue and 2 lavender flowers. The peach flowers have light peach petals and medium peach centers. Appliqué bias stems first, then L2 leaves. Next appliqué A petals and C centers.

2. Sew the 12 appliquéd blocks together.

3. Referring to the Border Placement Diagram, complete appliqué on borders, except for the corner flowers, which will be appliquéd after the borders have been sewn to the blocks. Flowers in the border are medium peach with dark peach centers. Buds are dark peach. Appliqué A petals for buds first, then B bud stems, L2 leaves, L1 leaves and flower stems. Last, appliqué A petals for flowers and C centers.

4. Sew short and long borders to the assembled blocks, mitering corner seams. Appliqué corner flowers.

5. Layer quilt top, batting and backing, then baste.

6. Quilt around all appliquéd pieces. A feathered wreath may be quilted in the center of each block. Fill remaining areas with diagonal lines.

7. Edge of quilt may be scalloped or left straight. Bind quilt with dark peach.

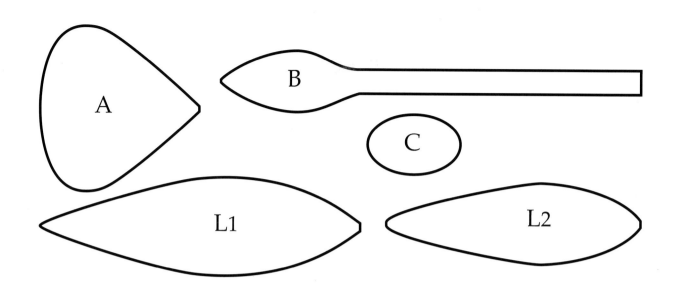

Border Placement Diagram

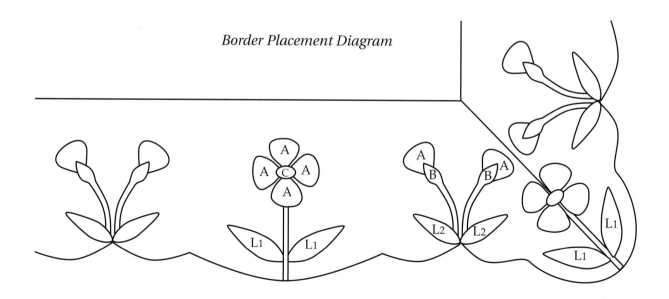

Block Placement Diagram

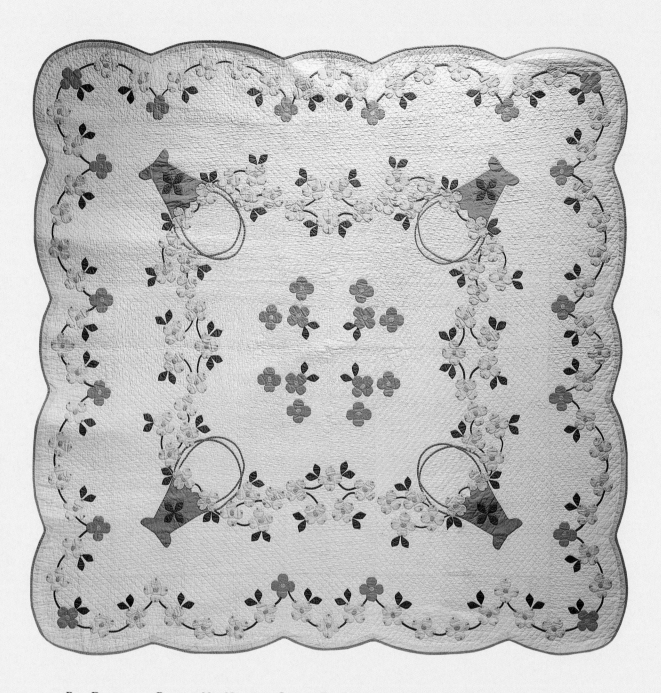

PINK DOGWOOD IN BASKETS. 83 X 83 INCHES. COTTON. DESIGNED AND APPLIQUÉD BY MARIE WEBSTER ABOUT 1927.
THE NAME OF THE QUILTER IS NOT KNOWN. THIS ROMANTIC DESIGN FEATURES BOTH DARK AND
LIGHT PINK DOGWOOD BLOSSOMS, WITH TINY PETAL TIPS IN CONTRASTING SHADES.
Collection of Katherine Webster Dwight.

Bursting into bloom after the long northern winter, the dogwood was a favorite of the Webster family. Like a breath of springtime, Pink Dogwood in Baskets is Marie's best known design of the late 1920s.

White Dogwood, her first dogwood pattern, was among her earliest quilts, published in the *Ladies' Home Journal* in 1912. Some fifteen years later, she was again inspired by the dogwood's beauty. "Pink Dogwood in Appliqué for the Bedroom" was featured in the *Ladies' Home Journal* of September 1927, pictured on a four-poster bed.

Embracing the Colonial Revival, the magazine extolled the virtues of handmade quilts and encouraged women to make their own heirlooms: "Our grandmothers were not the only ones whose homes could boast handmade bedquilts of intriguing color and design! Everyone today can have an equal claim to glory and without too much labor or too much money outlay either."

PINK DOGWOOD IN BASKETS

In this strong design, reminiscent of Magpie Rose, four large baskets anchor the corners of the quilt. Light pink flowers tumble out of the baskets to form a large wreath, surrounding a neat arrangement of dark pink blooms in the center. In the border, garlands of light and dark blossoms echo the curves of the scalloped edges.

The quilt is made from blocks of different sizes, a distinctive feature of many Webster designs. The four square basket blocks, Block a, are the largest, and alternate with narrow rectangular blocks, Block b. In the center is one small square block, Block c, containing just four flowers with their leaves.

As in many of her quilts, Marie varied the geometric quilting designs to define different parts of the quilt. She placed double diagonals inside the wreath, diamonds between the wreath and the border garland, and single diagonals extending out toward the edge of the quilt. The narrow pink border was left unquilted.

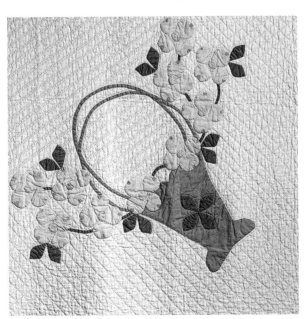

" The old and the new meet on common ground in this appliquéd quilt with its charming design of dogwood blossoms. For the fascinating quilt... is as easy to make as it is delightful to look at, and anyone who knows the rudiments of sewing can fashion one like it. "

LADIES' HOME JOURNAL, SEPTEMBER 1927

PINK DOGWOOD IN BASKETS *pattern*

Quilt: 87½″ x 87½″

Blocks:

four blocks 25½″ x 25½″

four blocks 13½″ x 25½″

one block 13½″ x 13½″

Border: 11½″ wide

(includes 1″ light pink border)

Binding: ¼″ wide

9 yards white for background and borders

2¾ yards light pink for flowers and border

1 yard dark pink for flowers

¼ yard yellow for flower centers

1 yard light green for baskets

1¾ yards dark green for leaves and stems

9 yards for backing

1 yard dark pink for binding

White
Cut 9 yards into 2 pieces:
  4 yards and 5 yards.
From 4 yards cut:
  4 squares 26″ x 26″
  4 squares 14″ x 26″
  1 square 14″ x 14″
Cut 5 yards into 2 pieces of 2½ yards.
From each piece, cut 2 borders 12″ x 88″.

Light pink
Cut 2¾ yards into 2 pieces:
  1¾ yards and 1 yard.
From 1¾ yards cut:
  240 A petals
  128 B petal tips
From 1 yard, cut bias strips 1½″ wide
  for border.

Dark pink
64 A petals
480 B petal tips

Yellow
152 C flower centers

Light Green
Cut 1 yard into 2 pieces of ½ yard.
From ½ yard, cut 4 D baskets.
From ½ yard, cut bias strips ¾″ wide
  for basket handles.

Dark Green
Cut 1¾ yards into 2 pieces:
  ¾ yard and 1 yard.
From ¾ yard, cut 176 L leaves.
From 1 yard, cut bias strips ¾″ wide
  for stems.

Backing
Cut 9 yards into three 3-yard pieces.
Seam lengthwise.

Binding
Cut bias strips 1¼″ wide for ¼″
finished single fold binding.

1. Referring to the Block Placement Diagrams, complete appliqué on 4 Block a, 4 Block b and 1 Block c. Each dogwood flower is made of 2 A petals, 4 B petal tips and one C center. Slip the petal tips underneath the notches of the petals, as shown on the A template.

Block a:
Appliqué bias stems and basket handles, then D baskets, L leaves and dogwood flowers.

Block b:
Appliqué bias stems, then L leaves and dogwood flowers.

Block c:
Appliqué L leaves, then dogwood flowers.

2. Referring to the Border Placement Diagram, complete appliqué on borders. Appliqué bias stems, then L leaves and dogwood flowers. The flowers and leaves at the corners will be appliquéd after the borders are sewn to the quilt top and the corners have been mitered.

3. Stitch the 9 appliquéd blocks together. Add appliquéd borders. Complete appliqué of flowers and leaves at the corners.

4. Appliqué light pink bias border onto white borders, scalloping edges if desired.

5. Layer quilt top, batting and backing, then baste.

6. Quilt around outside of all appliquéd pieces. Quilt remaining areas as desired.

7. Bind quilt with dark pink.

Block c

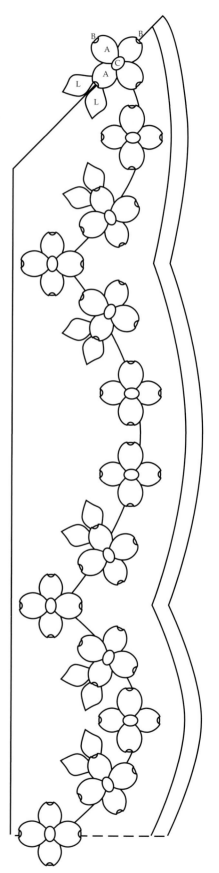

Block a

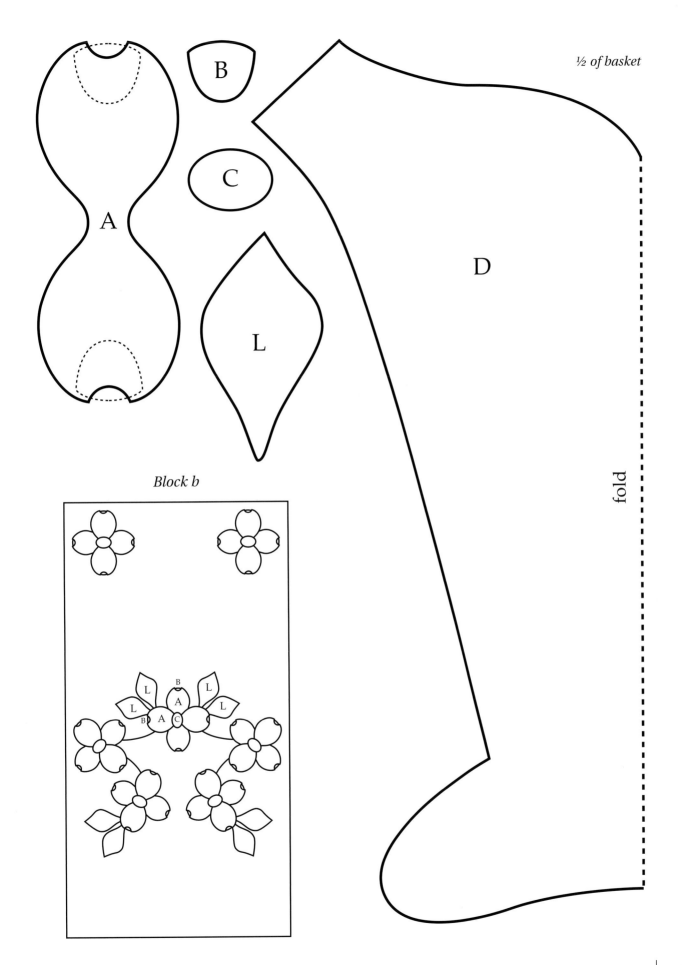

½ of basket

B

C

A

L

D

fold

Block b

RAINBOW. 68 x 93 INCHES. COTTON. DESIGNED BY MARIE WEBSTER IN THE LATE 1920S.
APPLIQUÉD BY MARIE WEBSTER, 1936. THE NAME OF THE QUILTER IS NOT KNOWN. THIS DESIGN IS NOTABLE
FOR ITS ART DECO-INSPIRED GEOMETRIC BORDER AND SIMPLIFIED FLOWER SHAPES.

Collection of Katherine Webster Dwight.

A burst of color transformed Marie Webster's last two quilt designs, Rainbow and Gay Garden. No longer content with a limited palette, she capped her designing career with an array of multi-colored blossoms.

The original color scheme for Rainbow was yellow, pink, blue, lavender and green. The quilt illustrated here shows off the bolder color choices of her daughter-in-law, Jeanette, who planned to make a pair of single bed quilts. When Jeanette found little time for sewing after the birth of her first child, Marie appliquéd the quilt tops and arranged to have them quilted by one of the excellent needlewomen she knew. Then Marie presented the finished quilts to her son and daughter-in-law as a surprise house-warming gift.

A pattern clearly derived from

RAINBOW

Rainbow was later sold by other pattern businesses under the name Spring Bouquet, with no acknowledgment of Marie Webster as the original designer. Then, renamed again, in 1933 it was sold by the Rural New Yorker as Daffodil and Trillium, one of their "old-fashioned quilt patterns." Their customers were probably blissfully unaware that this "old-fashioned" pattern had been designed only five years earlier!

The bouquets in Rainbow may have inspired the Nancy Page Quilt Club pattern, French Bouquet, published in 1933. This series pattern by Florence La Ganke showed 12 different bouquets, each tied with an extravagant bow. While the bouquets included a variety of different flowers, the trillium was virtually identical to the three-petaled flower in Rainbow.

*" The reward of [the quilter's] work lies, not only in the pleasure of doing,
but also in the joy of possession – which can be passed on even to future generations,
for a well-made quilt is a lasting treasure."*

MARIE WEBSTER, QUILTS: THEIR STORY AND HOW TO MAKE THEM

115

RAINBOW *pattern*

FINISHED SIZES

Quilt: 70″ x 94″

Blocks: 16″ x 18″

Border widths:

5″ white

1″ green

1″ lavender

1¼″ dark peach

1¼″ blue

1½″ dark peach

Binding: ¼″ wide

YARDAGE

6 yards white for background and borders

2¾ yards lavender for petals and borders

⅛ yard dark lavender for flower centers

2¾ yards blue for petals and borders

⅛ yard dark blue for flower centers

¾ yard peach for petals

2¾ yards dark peach for petals, flower centers, bars and borders

2¾ yards green for leaves, stems and borders

6 yards for backing

¾ yard dark peach for binding

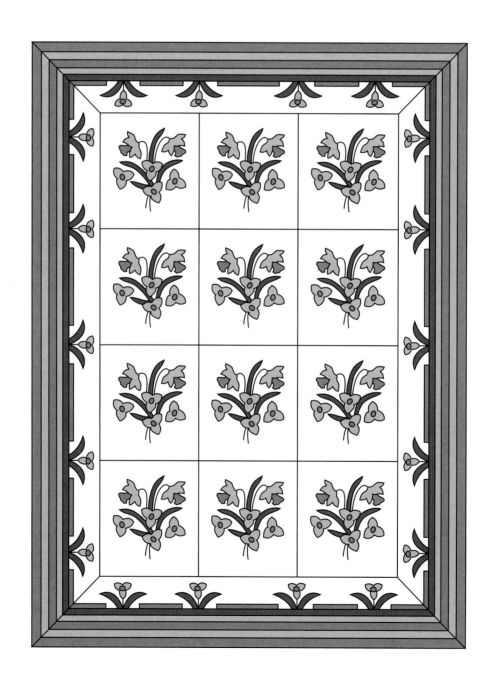

White
Cut 6 yards into 2 pieces: 3½ yards and 2½ yards.
From 3½ yards, cut 12 rectangles 16½″ x 18½″.
From 2½ yards cut:
    2 borders 5½″ x length of fabric
    2 borders 5½″ x length of fabric

Lavender
4 borders 1½″ x length of fabric
12 D petals, 9 E petals

Dark lavender
21 C flower centers

Blue
4 borders 1¾″ x length of fabric
24 D petals, 9 E petals

Dark blue
33 C flower centers

Peach
12 D petals, 24 E petals

Dark peach
4 borders 1¾″ x length of fabric
4 borders 2″ x length of fabric
3 strips 1¼″ x length of fabric for bars, then cut:
    8 bars 6½″
    4 bars 7½″
    4 bars 9½″
    2 bars 10½″
    4 bars 12½″
24 B petals
12 C flower centers

Green
4 borders 1½″ x length of fabric
12 L1 leaves
12 L2 leaves
12 L3 leaves and 12 L3 leaves reversed
18 L4 leaves and 18 L4 leaves reversed
Cut ¾″ wide bias strips for stems

Backing
Cut 6 yards into two 3-yard pieces. Seam lengthwise.

Binding
Cut bias strips 1¼″ wide for ¼″ finished single fold binding.

1. Referring to the Placement Diagram, complete appliqué on 12 blocks. Each block has 2 daffodils with A and B petals in peach and 4 trilliums (1 peach, 2 blue, and 1 lavender) with D petals and C centers . First, appliqué bias stems, then L1 leaves, L2 leaves, L3 leaves and L3 leaves reversed. Appliqué B petals, then A petals. Appliqué D petals, then C centers.

2. Referring to the Placement Diagram, complete appliqué on white borders. Lavender and blue trilliums with E petals and C centers alternate in the borders. Appliqué bias stems first, then L4 leaves and L4 leaves reversed. Appliqué E petals and C flower centers. Appliqué three sides of each bar onto white borders. The fourth side will be caught in the seam with the green border.

3. Stitch the narrow borders together lengthwise in the following order: 1½″ green, 1½″ lavender, 1¾″ dark peach, 1¾″ blue, 2″ dark peach. Sew pieced border units to appliquéd borders. Trim 2 borders to 70½″ and 2 borders to 94½″.

4. Stitch the 12 appliquéd blocks together. Add border units to blocks, mitering the corner seams.

5. Layer quilt top, batting and backing, then baste.

6. Quilt around outside of all appliquéd pieces. Fill remaining areas as desired.

7. Bind quilt.

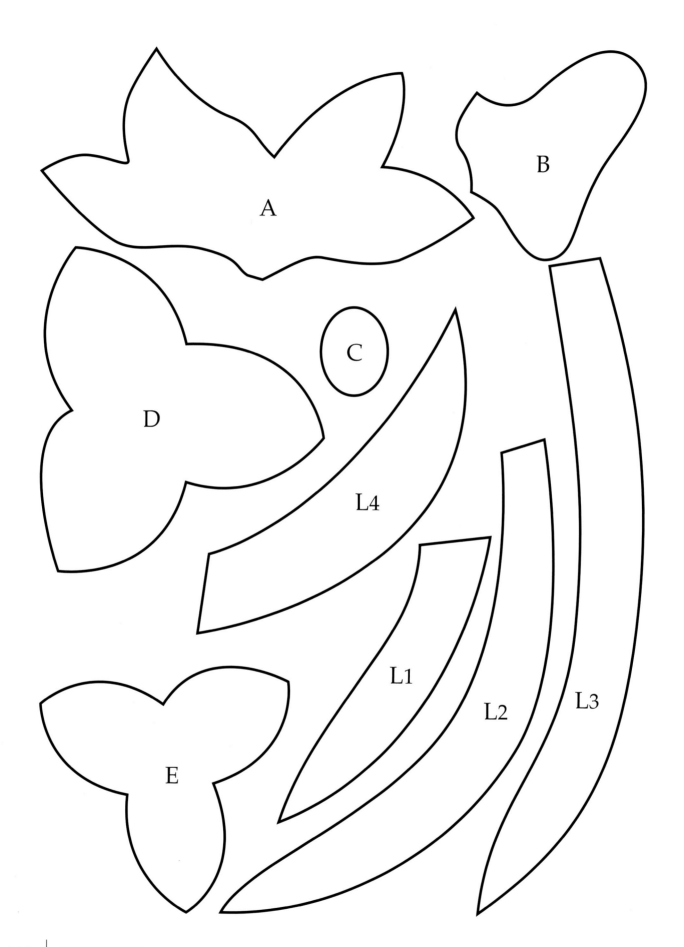

A

B

C

D

L4

L1

L2

L3

E

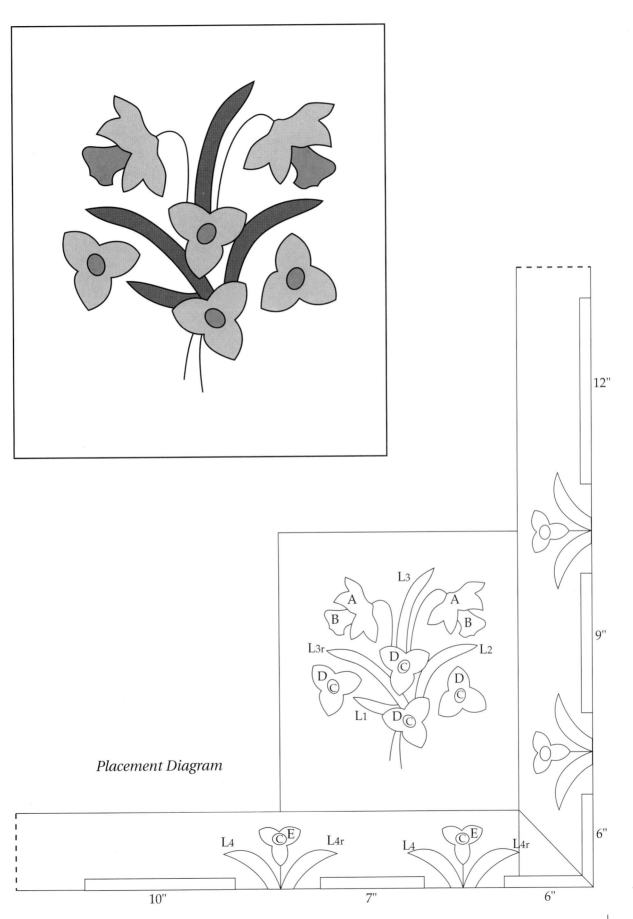

Placement Diagram

L3

A

B

A

B

L3r

D

D
C

L2

C

D

C

D
C

L1

12"

9"

6"

L4

C E

L4r

L4

C E

L4r

10"

7"

6"

GAY GARDEN. 78 x 89 INCHES. COTTON. DESIGNED AND APPLIQUÉD BY MARIE WEBSTER ABOUT 1929.
THE NAME OF THE QUILTER IS UNKNOWN. LIKE MANY WEBSTER QUILTS, THIS ONE BOASTS A DISTINCTIVE BORDER.
Collection of Rosamond S. Eliassen.

Gay Garden is the most colorful of Marie Webster's quilts. What a contrast with the muted palettes of her early work!

This bright and cheerful design was her last, dating from about 1929. While the blossoms are extremely simple, the overall design is complex and sophisticated, making the flowers seem to dance across the surface of the quilt. Curving stems intertwine at the center of each large block, while a secondary pattern of floral wreaths is created where the blocks meet. Marie has designed an original border treatment, echoing the curving border vine.

Like most Webster designs, this one inspired a number of variations sold by other pattern companies. A similar pattern known as Meadow Daisy appeared in the 1930s and 1940s, with Marie's three-petaled flowers transformed into four- and five-petaled daisies. As recently as the 1970s, J.P. Stevens and Co. sold a set of sheets and pillowcases called "Jessica's Quilt," whose design was obviously copied from a Gay Garden quilt.

We hope you've enjoyed this collection of timeless patterns. We invite you to share with us a picture of your completed quilt. For nearly a century, Marie Webster's quilt designs have embodied the motto adopted by the Practical Patchwork Company, "A Thing of Beauty is a Joy Forever." We trust they will continue to bring joy for at least another hundred years!

GAY GARDEN

"A thing of beauty is a joy for ever:
Its loveliness increases; it will never
Pass into nothingness; but still will keep
A bower quiet for us, and a sleep
Full of sweet dreams..."

JOHN KEATS, *ENDYMION*

GAY GARDEN *pattern*

FINISHED SIZES

Quilt: 86″ x 98″

Blocks: 22″ x 26″

Borders: 10″ wide

Binding: ¼″ wide

YARDAGE

10 yards white for background and borders

1¼ yards light pink for petals

¾ yard dark pink for petals

1½ yards light lavender for petals

¾ yard dark lavender for petals

1¾ yards blue for petals

1¾ yards yellow for petals and flower centers

⅛ yard orange for flower centers

1¾ yard green for leaves and stems

9 yards for backing

¾ yard green for binding

White
Cut 10 yards into 2 pieces:
  7 yards and 3 yards.
From 7 yards, cut 9 rectangles 22½″ x 26½″.
From 3 yards, cut:
  2 borders 10½″ x 86½″
  2 borders 10½″ x 98½″

Light pink
72 A petals

Dark pink
36 A petals

Light lavender
54 A petals
36 B petals

Dark lavender
27 A petals

Blue
81 A petals
36 B petals

Yellow
108 B petals
114 C flower centers

Orange
36 C flower centers

Green
Cut 1¾ yards into 2 pieces: 1 yard and ¾ yard.
From 1 yard cut:
  18 L1 leaves and 18 L1 leaves reversed
  46 L2 leaves and 46 L2 leaves reversed
From ¾ yard, cut ¾ wide bias strips
  for stems.

Backing
Cut 9 yards into three 3-yard pieces.
Seam lengthwise.

Binding
Cut bias strips 1¼″ wide for ¼″ finished single
fold binding.

1. Referring to the Placement Diagram, complete appliqué on nine blocks. Each block has 4 pink, 3 blue, and 3 lavender flowers. Each flower in the blocks contains 3 A petals and a yellow C center.

Appliqué bias stems first, then L1 leaves and L2 leaves. Appliqué A petals and then C centers.

2. Referring to the Placement Diagram, complete appliqué on borders. Each border has 8 yellow, 2 blue and 2 lavender flowers. Each corner has 1 yellow, 1 blue and 1 lavender flower. Each flower in the border contains 3 B petals. Yellow flowers have orange C centers, blue and lavender flowers have yellow C centers.

Appliqué bias stems first, then L2 leaves. Appliqué B petals then C centers. Do not appliqué the corner flower groups until after the borders have been joined to the blocks and the corner seams have been mitered.

3. Referring to the full quilt diagram, stitch together the nine appliquéd blocks. Add borders to blocks, mitering the corner seams. Complete appliqué at the corners. The outside edge of the borders may be left straight or blocked.

4. Layer quilt top, batting and backing, then baste.

5. Quilt around outside of all appliquéd pieces. Fill remaining areas as desired.

6. Bind quilt with green.

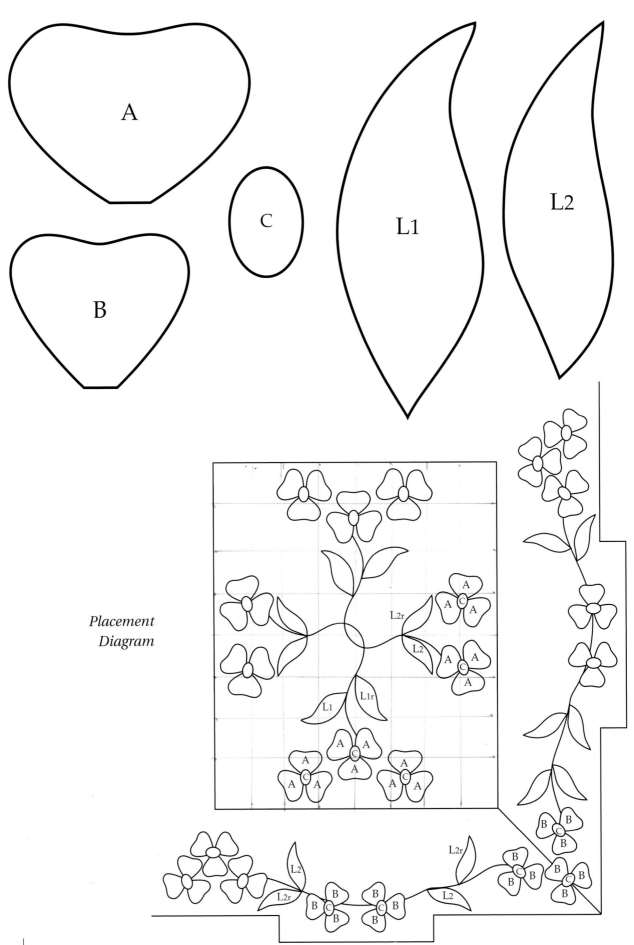

A

B

C

L1

L2

*Placement
Diagram*

QUILT PATTERNS AND KITS
DESIGNED BY MARIE WEBSTER

P – pattern   K – kit   J – pattern is in *A Joy Forever*   G – pattern is in *Marie Webster's Garden of Quilts*

Ladies' Home Journal, Jan. 1, 1911

P, G	American Beauty Rose
P, J	Iris
P	Snowflake
P, G	Wind Blown Tulip

Ladies' Home Journal, Jan. 1912

P, K, J	Poppy
P, K, G	Morning Glory
P, J	White Dogwood
P, J	Sunflower

Ladies' Home Journal, Aug. 1912

P, G	Pansies & Butterflies
P, J	Sunbonnet Lassies
P, J	Daisy
P	Wild Rose
P, G	Morning Glory Wreath
P, K, J	Bedtime

Designed between 1912 and 1919

P, J	Bunnies
P, J	Grapes & Vines
P	Daffodils & Butterflies
P	French Baskets with Daisies
P, K, J	French Baskets with Roses
P, K, G	Wreath of Roses
P, G	Cherokee Rose
P, J	Poinsettia
P, G	Magpie Rose
P	Nasturtium Wreath
P	Clematis in Bloom

Designed between 1920 and 1930

P, K, G	Cluster of Roses
K	Cluster of Roses spread
P, K, G	Dutch Basket
K	Dutch Basket spread
P, K, J	May Tulips
P, K	Iris in Baskets
P, K, G	Primrose Wreath
P, K, G	Pink Dogwood
P, K	Wayside Roses
P, K, G	Rainbow
P, K, G	Gay Garden

NASTURTIUM WREATH
78 x 89 INCHES. DESIGNED AND APPLIQUÉD BY MARIE WEBSTER. THE NAME OF THE QUILTER IS NOT KNOWN. ALTHOUGH THE DESIGN DATES FROM ABOUT 1920, THE QUILT WAS MADE SOME TEN YEARS LATER. NOTE THE ORIGINAL USE OF LEAVES TO FORM THE SCALLOPED BORDER. *Collection of Katherine Webster Dwight.*

Suggested Reading

Marie Webster and Her Times

Benberry, Cuesta. "Marie D. Webster: A Major Influence on Quilt Design in the 20th Century." *Quilter's Newsletter Magazine*, no. 224 (July/Aug. 1990), pp. 32-35.

—. "Marie Webster: Indiana's Gift to American Quilts." In *Quilts of Indiana: Crossroads of Memories*. Indiana Quilt Registry Project, Inc., Indiana University Press, 1991.

Nickols, Pat L. "Mary A. McElwain: Quilter and Quilt Businesswoman." In *Uncoverings 1991*. Edited by Laurel Horton. American Quilt Study Group, 1992, pp. 98-117.

Perry, Rosalind Webster, and Marty Frolli. *A Joy Forever: Marie Webster's Quilt Patterns*. Practical Patchwork, 1992.

Shankel, Carol, editor. *American Quilt Renaissance: Three Women Who Influenced Quiltmaking in the Early 20th Century*. Tokyo, Japan: Kokusai Art, 1997.

Waldvogel, Merikay. *Soft Covers for Hard Times: Quiltmaking and The Great Depression*. Rutledge Hill Press, 1990.

—. "The Origin of Mountain Mist Patterns." In *Uncoverings 1995*. Edited by Virginia Gunn. American Quilt Study Group, 1995, pp. 95-138.

Webster, Marie D. *Quilts: Their Story and How to Make Them*. (1915). Biography of the author by Rosalind Webster Perry. Practical Patchwork, 1990.

Appliqué and Quilting

Andreatta, Pat. *Appliqué Can Be Easy*. Heirloom Stitches, 1988.

Cory, Pepper. *Mastering Quilt Marking*. C. & T. Publishing, 1999.

Dietrich, Mimi. *Basic Quiltmaking Techniques for Hand Appliqué*. Martingale & Co., Inc., 1998.

—. *Basic Quiltmaking Techniques for Borders and Bindings*. Martingale & Co., Inc.,1999.

Fons, Marianne and Liz Porter. *Quilter's Complete Guide*. Oxmoor House, 1993.

Leone, Diana and Cindy Walter. *Fine Hand Quilting*. Krause Publications, second edition, 2000.

McClun, Diana and Laura Nownes. *Quilts! Quilts!! Quilts!!! The Complete Guide to Quiltmaking*. The Quilt Digest Press, second edition, 1997.

Simms, Ami. *How to Improve Your Quilting Stitch*. Mallery Press, 1987.

Sinema, Laurene. *Appliqué! Appliqué!! Appliqué!!! The Complete Guide to Hand Appliqué*. The Quilt Digest Press, 1995.

INDEX

PUBLICATIONS FROM
PRACTICAL PATCHWORK

A JOY FOREVER: MARIE WEBSTER'S QUILT PATTERNS

BY ROSALIND WEBSTER PERRY AND MARTY FROLLI

The first book of Marie Webster's appliqué quilt designs, featuring 12 original patterns from the early 1900s: French Baskets, Grapes & Vines, Iris, May Tulips, Poinsetia, Poppy, Sunflower, White Dogwood, and for baby – Bedtime, Bunnies, Daisy, and Sunbonnet Lassies.

96 pages, softcover, $19.50

1992, ISBN 0-9620811-7-5

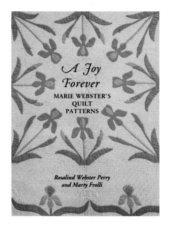

QUILTS: THEIR STORY AND HOW TO MAKE THEM

BY MARIE D. WEBSTER

Reprint of American's first quilt book, originally published in 1915. Complete original text and illustrations, with additional illustrations, biography of the author by Rosalind Webster Perry, notes, bibliography and index.

380 pages, softcover, $20

1990, ISBN: 0-9620811-6-7

MARIE WEBSTER'S GARDEN OF QUILTS

BY ROSALIND WEBSTER PERRY AND MARTY FROLLI

The second book of Webster patterns, sequel to *A Joy Forever,* with 14 different patterns.

128 pages, softcover, $25

2001, ISBN: 0-9620811-8-3

You may order these titles from the publisher.
Shipping and handling: one book $3, each additional book $1.
California residents, please add sales tax.
We accept Visa and Mastercard.

PRACTICAL PATCHWORK

P.O. Box 30065, Santa Barbara, CA 93130

Fax and phone: (805) 682-3664   *e-mail:* rperry@west.net

Visit our web site: www.mariewebster.net